Short Stories, Childhood Anecdotes and Simple Poems for Everyone

JULIAN LORENZANA

authorHOUSE®

AuthorHouse™
1663 Liberty Drive
Bloomington, IN 47403
www.authorhouse.com
Phone: 1 (800) 839-8640

Published by AuthorHouse 07/27/2018

ISBN: 978-1-5462-5269-6 (sc)
ISBN: 978-1-5462-5268-9 (e)

Library of Congress Control Number: 2018908740

Print information available on the last page.

*Any people depicted in stock imagery provided by Getty Images are models,
and such images are being used for illustrative purposes only.
Certain stock imagery* © *Getty Images.*

This book is printed on acid-free paper.

SYNOPSIS

"Short Stories, Childhood Anecdotes and Simple Poems for Everyone" contains four stories. In one, a little girl is traumatized by two auto accidents that claimed the lives of all her relatives. From the Los Niños Receiving Home she attends school and she is bullied. Because becomes rebellious at school and at her foster homes, she is returned to Los Niños. Finally, a school friend invites her to live with her family and her existence becomes more pleasant. She eventually graduates from college with a teaching credential and soon marries her prince charming. Another story deals with a hate-love feud between classmates that ends up in matrimony. In the next two stories, children and adults are taught that heeding advice can help avoid unpleasant consequences.

Finally, the anecdotes and the poems listed are mainly personal experiences expressed in prose or in simple rhyme for everyone to fully understand and enjoy.

CONTENTS

A NEED TO BELONG

By
Julian Lorenzana

I was dozing off on the couch waiting for my husband to return from work and I must have fallen asleep. Suddenly, I heard the doorbell ringing and a knocking on the door. That knocking sent my mind back to the two times a police officer rang our doorbell and gave us the terrible news that my grandparents, my father, my mother and my stepfather had been killed in auto accidents. The events were so real in my mind that I did not realize I was having a nightmare.

"Why, God? Why did you do this to me? Why did you take my grandparents, and now my mother and my stepfather? What have I done so bad that you had to punish me by taking the only family I had?" I wailed

As Lois, my foster mother, walked by my room, she heard my outburst and my inconsolable wailing. She knocked on the door and I opened it right away.

"Lina, what's wrong? Why are crying and asking God so many questions? You're sad and angry because God took your relatives away, right?" Lois asked.

"Yes, I am, Mrs. Hartford!" I answered. "I'm sad and angry at Him for doing this to me! I keep hearing that He takes people for a reason but I can't see what reason he had for leaving me all alone in this world!" I added.

I had been living with my first foster parents, Frederick and Lois Hartford, for a few days and I tried to get along with them but it was difficult because I had been so happy before my mother and my stepfather were killed. Now, all I felt was anger at God, at the world, and a little bit at Lois after she told me, "They say a person dies because God wants him or her with Him and to find out how those he or she leaves behind take that loss."

"But I don't know of anybody who loses all her relatives, leaving her all alone. He left me all alone. That's what makes it so hard to understand. I don't know how adults can handle a loss better than children. Maybe it's because they are grown up. But me! How does God expect me to know what to do? I'm just a little girl!" I exclaimed and began to cry again, but this time quietly.

Lois simply hugged me and told me, "You will know what to do. You'll be sad and possibly angry for some time but in a few years, when you think about them, you may still be sad but you'll feel better."

After Lois left me alone, I felt a little better but shortly thereafter, a short period of depression set in as I tried to figure out why I had to live with foster parents. I began to recall the steps that had brought me to live with Frederick and Lois.

My mother, Julianne, was the only child of Richard and Connie Pelozzi and she grew up under very strict rules of parenting. This fact is probably the cause of some of the disagreements between them. She was not allowed to do some of the things children like to do, such as visiting with friends, taking part in sleep-overs, spending time on the phone and many others. This overprotection turned her into a rebellious child.

At the age of 16, because of this suffocating parenting, my mother decided to run away with her boyfriend, my father John. Her parents were furious but they kept in touch. A year later, after she told her parents that she was pregnant, they made peace with her and invited both John and her to move in with them.

Life became happier for Julianne as she had more freedom to do whatever she wanted, with John's approval. All of them shared the same activities. They went everywhere together. My grandparents were happy doing things with my mom and dad, showering them with all kinds of conveniences. Later, they were thrilled with their approaching marriage.

Soon, the happy event came and the entire neighborhood shared in the happy event. It was not a church ceremony. A judge married them in front of only close family and friends. The music at the dance hall was provided by a local DJ and everyone present had a great time, especially the newlyweds.

Eight months later, on October 12, 1939, I was born, to the delight of the whole family. I, supposedly, brought a ray of happiness not seen in the Pelozzi family for a long time. And that happiness lasted for a long time as I became the heart of the family. According to my mother, I was very smart and outgoing, always entertaining with my antics.

At the age of eleven, my happiness was shattered when my grandparents and my father took a trip to the nearest big city. On their way back, they encountered a drunk driver on the road. The drunk driver supposedly tried to pass them and as he turned to the left lane to pass them, his car got too close to them. In attempts to avoid being hit, my grandfather swerved to the right a little too much and when he tried to straighten his car, the car flipped over on its side and it rolled into the canal running parallel to the road. When help arrived, my grandparents and my father were found dead.

This tragic event was so much for me that I went into a period of depression. I had been so happy and now my mother and I were left to fend for ourselves. It was hard for us to get over our loss.

When my mother finally got a job, our lives improved tremendously but our hearts were still bleeding. Soon, though, Mom met Stephen, who swept her off her feet. I was now twelve years old so I wasn't too happy about my father being replaced by a new man but I soon was won over by Stephen. The way he treated me and my mother showed me that he was a good man. Almost everywhere Mom and he went, I was allowed to tag along.

A few months later, my mom and Stephen got married and we lived happily as a family. I was now thirteen years old and I couldn't be happier with my mother and my stepfather. We got along so well that he decided to adopt me as his own daughter. For that reason, he and my mother took a trip to Los Angeles. They planned to buy me a surprise gift. I was left behind because three of my classmates and I had made a date to spend the day at my house.

Around noon, on June 18, 1952, I received a call from my mother and Stephen telling me that they were on their way home and I was full of expectations. I was really excited and anxious to find out what the surprise was. My friends, Mary, Rosie and Julie, were listening in on the phone conversation, as I had the phone on speaker, and they were sharing my excitement. My mother told me they would be home around three o'clock. My friends and I went back to our activities and we kept looking at the wall clock off and on with great anxiety.

At two thirty, the phone rang again and we ran to answer it. My friends kept their eyes on me, watching the elation mirrored on my face. When my face paled with shock, they became worried and in unison they asked, "What on earth happened? What's wrong? You're ready to cry!"

"It's the police!" I shouted as I put the phone down and started to cry. "My mother and Stephen were in an accident! They're dead! Oh, my God! What am I going to do now? I don't have anybody now. I'm all alone!" I complained as I cried even louder.

The three girls quickly tried to soothe the awful feeling I felt by telling me, "We're awfully sorry, Lina. But you are not alone! You have us. We'll help you in any way we can. Everything will be all right. You'll see."

No matter how hard they tried, I continued crying inconsolably as I said, "Oh, God! Why me? Why me? I was so happy after all that mourning for my grandparents and my father! Why did you take them away from me? Now there's nothing left for me! I want to die, too!" I complained between sobs.

My parents' bodies were brought home and my neighbors came to the rescue. While I kept to myself, my neighbors and some county personnel made the arrangements for the funeral. The arms of grief and depression engulfed me to

3

the point where I didn't even make an appearance at the wake or at the burial ceremony. Both times, I stayed at home under the care of two county workers who desperately tried to console me.

Against my wishes, I was taken to Los Niños Receiving Home, where children without relatives or whose parents or guardians can't discipline them are placed. I was to remain there until foster parents could be found.

While at Los Niños, I attended school at El Centro's junior high school. I was thirteen years old and in the seventh grade. The loss of my parents and grandparents had hardened me to the point where I began showing some negative characteristics. I couldn't make friends. I preferred to keep to myself. I became distrustful because I thought everybody was against me. I got into arguments frequently and sometimes those arguments led to fights that landed me in the principal's office. The only girls who could be called my friends were my classmates, Terrie and Carol. They were considered loners themselves so we didn't see each other too often.

Henry Elmore and his wife, Lana, had been married for 15 years and they had not been able to have children so when they learned of my plight, they offered to take me in. They went through the usual routine of rules and regulations and they were found to be very good candidates for foster parenting. They met me and both they and I decided to give it a try.

For three months, we got along fairly well. I felt good as they pampered me a lot, trying to drive away my moments of sadness and win me over at the same time. This was during the summer months so we did a lot of things together. We went out together and we watched my favorite TV programs together. It seemed as if everything was working out well for us as a family until the school year began.

I was now 14 years old and in the eighth grade. While I was living at Los Niños, I had attended school in El Centro. But now that I was going to live in Brawley, I would have to attend school at Barbara Worth Junior High School. I hoped to graduate from the eighth grade this year.

When classes began, I found myself in room 21 with Mr. John Russell as my teacher. I was new in Brawley so I didn't know anybody and I wished my three friends, Mary, Rosie and Julie, were here with me but they were attending junior high school in El Centro. I felt uncomfortable the first day because I thought everybody was staring at me so I decided to block them out of my mind. My trick did not work because I began to think about my father, my grandparents, my mother and my stepfather and tears began to roll down my cheeks. And when I began to sob, I really became the center of attention. Mr. Russell and two classmates went to me and tried to find out what was wrong.

"Your name is Lina, right? asked Mr. Russell.

"Yes," I answered meekly.

"What is the matter? Why are you crying?" he inquired. "You should be happy. This is the first day of school and in about a year you'll be a freshman in high school" he added. "If you're afraid of your teacher, I don't think I'm a monster," he assured me. "You'll see. We'll get along well," he added.

"Oh, no, Mr. Russell, I'm not crying because of that. They've told me you are a very good and well-liked teacher. I'm simply remembering my mother, my stepfather and my grandparents. I lost them very recently and it makes me real sad when I think about them," I explained. "I'm sorry. I feel as if I'm all alone in the world and I can't help feeling sorry for myself," I added.

"You're not alone, Lina," interrupted a classmate. "My name is Sophie. You have your foster parents and everybody in this classroom. I'm sorry about your loss. I understand your sorrow because my brother died last year and I still feel sad at times. We're all behind you," she promised.

"She's right," piped in Luana, another classmate. "I don't know how we can help you but we'll find a way. By the end of the year you'll have many friends and you will be a happier person. My mother always tells me, 'Time heals all wounds'," she added.

"Thank you all for your good intentions. My grandmother used to tell me the same thing. I know you're trying to drive my pain away but, right now, it seems impossible to me," I stated.

"Well, this conversation did some good because you're not crying anymore. We know you're still sad inside and the sadness will remain with you for a long time. We also know that, eventually, we'll find out that Luana and your grandmother were right about time healing all wounds," Mr. Russell injected.

For days, Mr. Russell noticed that I had some moments of sadness. I hardly ever joined in when he brought up a subject for class discussion. He called on me to share my ideas or opinions about the topics but I usually didn't know what to say. To him, it meant that I had not been paying attention.

The days, weeks and months rolled by and I became even more aloof. I kept to myself, despite some girls' attempts at making friends with me.

One day, a girl named Liz approached me and told me, "Hey, Lina, I hear you're all alone. What happened to your parents? Did they leave you because you're too hard to get along?" I got real angry but I simply gave her a dirty look and said, "I don't know. God simply took them," and I walked away, leaving her standing there.

Three days later, I was standing by myself out in the playground when Liz and two of her friends approached me again. I tried to ignore them but Liz started talking, "I was told that your relatives were drunk and that was why they were involved in an accident and got killed. Do you drink, too? You'd better not drive when you get your first car or you'll end up like your parents."

My temper flared up and I answered with, "It's none of your business if I drink or not drink! Maybe you're the one who drinks and are loaded right now. You would not be looking for trouble if you were sober!"

Liz couldn't take my retort so she lunged forward and tried to slap me but I was able to grab her wrist and give it a strong twist making her moan with pain. She, again, lunged at me and this time we grabbed each other's arms. Our struggle took us to the ground where we wrestled, trying to take the upper hand. A crowd gathered around us and many egged us on, some taking sides.

The fight didn't last long because the commotion brought two teachers to the melee and they were able to separate us. They stopped the fight but not before issuing a warning about detention.

Before I was called to the office, I met Leslie, who is in the same grade. I was sitting at a bench near the cafeteria when she approached me. She introduced herself, "Hello, Lina. My name is Leslie and, seeing that you're alone, I decided to visit with you. I'm not here to irritate you in any way. In fact, I'm here to try to tell you that I was a distance away from you when those girls came to you to cause trouble. I didn't come closer but I heard everything they said to you. Kids have always bullied me so I try to stay by myself, away from crowds, so I won't get into trouble. In other words, I'm a loner, probably like you. I've noticed that you sit alone often so I assumed that you like to stay away from crowds, too. I know that sometimes bullies seek other kids to bully them. I have also found out that if someone has it out for you, he or she will seek you out. I've gotten into trouble that way. Anyway, I'm sure they will call you into the office to explain why you were fighting. And before they do, I decided to tell you that I'm willing to tell who started the fight. Okay?"

"Okay, and thanks, Leslie," I said. "I hope I don't need to get you involved in this because there may be reprisals against you," she added.

Leslie and I had a long and pleasant conversation, talking about things of interest to fourteen-year olds. We did not bring out the subject of family. When the bell rang announcing the next class period, we went to our next class but not before we said, "See you later and nice meeting you," to each other.

A lot of my classmates must have known all about my grandparents, my parents and my stepfather because they read the newspapers or because their parents told them about the accidents that took their lives. Some, especially girls, were out to get more facts from me or simply to cause some trouble for me. Many tried to befriend me and they succeeded. Though I had some friends, other girls constantly harassed me with questions that hurt me. I had several encounters that landed me in the principal's office and I even became rebellious with some of my teachers. All those incidents were too overwhelming and, for that reason, I was absent from school very often. School personnel and care workers made several trips to my house to talk to Mr. and Mrs. Elmore, my foster parents. There, they learned that I had become rebellious and that they couldn't handle me. As a result, I was returned to Los Niños, a place I had learned to hate.

Once back at Los Niños, I tried to comply with the rules and regulations and to make myself at home but I couldn't. I broke some rules and I was punished often by grounding me. There were many activities I had enjoyed before but I couldn't participate in them anymore. I had tasted life on the outside of Los Niños and I thought I would rather live with foster parents, even if I had to abide by the rules governing the foster home family.

I was soon taken to live with my second foster family, Mary and Joe Sanders, who had two sons. Again, everything went very well for weeks but I soon found out that the boys didn't like me. Apparently, Mary and Joe never asked the boys what they thought about me coming to live with them. Also, instead of dividing the chores among the three of us, Mrs. Sanders assigned all of them to me and I didn't like that at all. I thought I was being worked too hard.

I returned to the same school and I got along very well with all my teachers, who occasionally took me aside to counsel me and praise me for my nice behavior.

My life with the Sanders continued, sometimes harmoniously and other times problematic. But soon, one of the boys, Joe, took a five-dollar bill his mother had laid on the bar without thinking of the consequences. When Mary asked her sons if one of them had taken it, Joe told her he had seen me taking it. Mrs. Sanders went to my room to talk to me.

"Lina, I put a five-dollar bill on the bar and when I tried to retrieve it, it was gone. Joe told me that he saw you taking it. Is that true?" she asked.

"No, I did not take it," I answered.

"Joe told me he saw you taking it," Mrs. Sanders insisted.

"Well, he lied to you! I did not take it, honest. I'm here as a guest. I wouldn't dare do something like that, I assure you," I argued. "It must have been one of the boys," I added.

"My boys have never stolen anything from me!" she retorted. "I'm sorry. I have to believe Jack was telling the truth. "I thought you were a good and honest girl but I guess I was wrong! We can't have you stealing money every time I put it down!" she shouted.

"But I did not take it! Honest! I don't know who could have taken it but it wasn't me! Why can't you believe me?" I asked, and immediately walked out.

One day, during a recess, a girl named Lana accosted me out on the playground. She was really angry! Apparently, she was jealous of me because she thought she had spotted me talking to her boyfriend, Tim. I denied it repeatedly to no avail because Lana lunged at me and threw me to the ground. A wrestling match ensued and, though I got the best of her, I took the brunt of the punishment. We were both taken to the principal's office, where we were asked to give our explanations.

The next day, our parents were called to the principal's office and we repeated our own version of the fight. Though I tried to explain that Lana had jumped me, my excuse fell on deaf ears. My foster parents sort of believed me but the principal didn't. My past experiences at school played a large part in who received the worst punishment. I was expelled from school for a week and Lana simply got a reprimand from the principal.

Because of my experiences at home with the Sanders and the apparent favoritism played by the principal, I requested to be sent back to Los Niños and my request was readily granted. Thus, my life with my second foster parents came to an abrupt halt.

Leslie was not aware of my latest incident in school so, one day, she went looking for me because she wanted to talk to me about her family. She spoke with one of my teachers, who told her about the latest problem she had had with me and the resulting consequences. Needless to say, Leslie was really sorry about what had happened to me. She was sorry she hadn't witnessed the fight. She thought she could have helped me if she had been one of the witnesses. Apparently she liked me, in spite of all my problems, and she decided to visit me at Los Niños.

Before Leslie went to see me, she had talked to her family about the problems I was going through. They knew what had happened to my relatives but she repeated the story to them. She thought I could come live with them so she asked her parents, "Dad and Mom, do you think Lina could come live with us? She has been at two foster homes but she hasn't been happy there. I think she needs somebody to identify with and there are three girls here. She is my age and she and I have hit it off. We are already friends but we could become more than friends. We could become sisters, for instance. Of course, we would be foster sisters if she were to come live with us. What do you say? If you want to we can go visit her at Los Niños. Perhaps she wouldn't want to come live with us but, at least, we would have made the attempt to help her. She's really a good girl but bad luck has constantly followed her."

"I don't know, Leslie," her dad answered. "Do you really want Lina to come live with us? She has gotten into so much trouble. Who's going to tell me that she won't continue on the same page? I know that losing one's loved ones is tough but it's about time she stopped making so much about her loss. What do you think, Tere?" he asked.

"I don't know, honey," she answered. "She must really be carrying great sorrow. Don't forget. Losing one's loved one is rough enough but she didn't lose just one. She lost four." she argued. "My goodness! I really feel sorry for her. So far, she hasn't lived with a family where she can interact with some one her own age and gender. We have three girls here who can help her make her life a little happier. I think she needs a chance and I would like to meet her and talk to her. But we should discuss this with Lily and Susan, too, she added.

"Of course, Tere. We have to hear what they think about having an extra sister," Mr. Lorenzana said.

At that instant, Susan and Lily came into the room and Susan asked, "Who's having an extra sister? What are you three talking about?"

"Yeah, I want to know, too. And who is this extra sister and whose sister is she going to be?" Lily asked.

"I met a girl at school named Lina who has had some problems at school. And those problems started after she had lost her mother and her stepfather. "First, her grandparents and her father were killed in a car accident and, just recently, she lost her mother and her stepfather in another car accident, leaving her without any relative to take care of her. Because of her recent behavior, caused by being bullied by some students, she was expelled from school, resulting in her going to Los Niños Receiving Home. She has been placed in two foster homes already and, apparently, she didn't last in either one for very long," Leslie explained.

"So what does that have to do with this extra sister you are talking about?" asked Lily.

"Well, she and I have become fairly good friends and I wish I could help her in some way. I suggested to Mom and Dad that our own home could become her next foster home. But, of course, we need your input," she declared. "What do you girls think of my idea?" she asked.

"I wouldn't mind," declared Susan. "But do we have enough room for her? We have only four bedrooms and they are all taken already," she added.

"I don't know if we will qualify as a foster home," declared Lily. "You know that people from the county will come to check us and our house, right?" she asked. "Of course, we don't lose anything if we don't qualify. But, at least, we will have tried to help Lina. And if we do qualify and she is willing to try us out, my bedroom is big enough for another bed. Of course, I'll end up losing my privacy but I wouldn't care. But it is all up to Mom and Dad," she continued.

"Your mom is very sympathetic toward Lina and she is willing to do it," her dad said. "But I don't know. I already have three girls I have to put up with and I don't know if adding another one would be too much," he added.

"What do you mean by 'I have to put up with'?" all three girls exclaimed simultaneously.

"I'm only kidding! You're three wonderful girls and I'm proud of you. Sure, we have our disagreements sometimes but nothing out of the ordinary," he said. "But let me think about it for a few days, okay, Leslie?" he requested.

"Okay, Dad. But please don't take too long or Lina may go to another foster home," Leslie replied.

Three days later, Mr. Lorenzana told Mrs. Lorenzana, "Poor girl! She has really been hit hard by tragedy and bad luck! And I agree that our three girls might be the medicine she needs to get out of her lonesome syndrome. And if she and the county accept us, may God illuminate and guide us in our attempts to help her."

The following day, when everyone was in the house, Mr. Lorenzana called them to the living room to announce his decision.

"Mom, girls," he said. I've thought this through and I've decided that it would be a terrible idea to........"

"Dad, what are you trying to tell us? Are you trying to tell us that you don't agree with us? Leslie interrupted.

"No!" he answered. "I'm simply trying to tell you that it would be terrible to let Lina navigate through life on her own. She's too young to let her sink into a worse situation," he corrected. "I deliberately took a pause to see how you would react," he explained. "I have decided to go along with your idea. I do feel sorry for what she's going through and I believe we may be able to help her. Let's just hope she and the county accept us. And if they do, may God, also, be with us on this because without Him we are bound to fail Lina," he continued. "We'll put in our application and visit her at the same time. I would like to meet her and speak with her. Let's hope it doesn't take long to get the county's reply. Her reply we will probably get when we visit her," he promised.

The next day, Mr. Lorenzana called the office of Los Niños and made an appointment to see Mrs. Johnson, the director. He was told that his wife and he could go see her the next day, at 10:30. When he asked if he had to fill out an application, he was told that the application could be made personally during their visit with Mrs. Johnson.

That same afternoon, Mr. and Mrs. Lorenzana went to school to pick up Leslie and, when they got there, they found Leslie and me conversing in the hall. Leslie introduced us and we crossed a few sentences. I must say I found them to be very pleasant to talk to. Needless to say, I liked them from the moment I met them.

The next day, at 10:30, all the Lorenzanas were in the director's office waiting for her. She soon came in and everything pertaining to the subject at hand was explained to them. She told them about the things they have to do in order to qualify as foster parents. Finally, Mrs. Johnson called me in.

After their daughters had exchanged some gossip with me, they were left alone with me. I'm almost sure they wanted to make sure I was at ease with them, but I was really nervous and I merely stared at them. Finally, I blurted out with a big smile, "So you want me to go live with you, huh?"

They were surprised because they had assumed that I knew nothing about the purpose of their visit. But thanks to my question, the air was cleared and our dialogue flowed smoothly.

"Well, since you already know the purpose of our visit, How would you like to go live with us?" Mr. Lorenzana asked.

"I don't know," I answered. "It would be neat! But I am not too good at controlling my temper. I've been to two foster homes and, for some reason, I wasn't able to get along with my foster parents. It's probably because of my temper," I added.

"Many of us have bad tempers but we learn to control it. If nobody had a bad temper, life would be dull, don't you think?" Mrs. Lorenzana asked.

"Hey, that's right! I guess I can learn to control my temper, too," I said. "Do your daughters have a bad temper?" I inquired.

"They all do," Mrs. Lorenzana answered. "But they are very sweet and gentle, just like you. That sweetness and gentleness makes up for their bad temper. And they have learned to control it," she added.

"What about your daughters? Do they want me to live with them, too? I asked.

"Of course. We all do," she assured me. "Who do you think suggested we should have you come live with us?" she asked.

"Was it Leslie?" I asked.

"Yes, it was Leslie," she answered. "You have not lived with a Mexican family and you may feel uncomfortable but we all think it is worth a try. We assure you, the language spoken at home is English. Once in a while, my wife and I do speak Spanish but not too often and not in front of the girls because they don't speak it. They understand some but they do not speak it. If you are unhappy with us after a while, you have the right to go live with somebody else. But we think you will be happy with us," she guaranteed.

"Man! It would be bad! The greatest!" I exclaimed ecstatically.

"I'll do it! Can you get me out of here today?" I asked.

"We would love to but, unfortunately, we'll have to wait a few days," Mr. Lorenzana answered. "Mrs. Johnson said she has to send some one to check our house. But I'm almost sure they will allow you to come live with us," she added. "As soon as the move is approved and they tell us to come pick you up, we'll be here as early and as quickly as possible," she promised.

"We will be greatly disappointed if you change your mind," Leslie told me. "No way, José! "I will be waiting for you!" she promised.

The hard knocking on the door finally woke me up from my deep sleep. Right away I realized it was probably my husband, so I got up and quickly opened the door.

"Sweetheart, what's wrong?" my husband asked. "You took forever to open the door and you are crying! Tell me why, please. You have me worried!" he added.

"Don't worry Richard. I'm all right. I just had a terrible dream. I think I heard the doorbell ringing but I must have been dreaming because when I opened the door, it was a police officer who had come to tell us that my grandparents, my father, my mother and my stepfather had been killed in auto accidents. From then on, my life story flashed through my mind like a bad movie. It was your hard knocking that finally woke me up. I'm sorry I took so long to open it," I apologized. "But why didn't you use your key?" I asked.

"I couldn't find it!" he answered. "But it's alright. It's okay now. Please stop crying. I know it's sad to recall those moments but that was a long time ago. Try to get over it for now. I don't want to dwell on your sad past but I need to ask you two more questions. Were you confident the Lorenzanas would go pick you up at the Los NiÑos Receiving Home after you spoke with them and they promised to pick you up as soon as they were approved?

"Yes, I was," I answered. "In fact, two weeks later, after all the requirements were met, the whole Lorenzana family went to pick me up and I finally set foot in their house. My life there was a little awkward for a few weeks. I wasn't sure I had made the right decision but after a while, I felt very much at home. Mr. and Mrs. Lorenzana were a little strict but they gave us many liberties. They were happy most of the time. They had a habit of singing every time they had nothing important to do and my three foster sisters usually joined them. Eventually, they convinced me to join them in most of their activities and I learned to love it," I admitted.

You told me your sad existence ended when you went to live with them. Can you tell me more about them?" Richard asked.

"Well, at first it was a little difficult because I felt like an outsider but that feeling didn't last long. They, too, included me in whatever they did. Don't get me wrong. Everything was not that easy. We had our differences but all siblings in a family have their problems," I explained. "But we all became a real family and we got along beautifully. We had great celebrations at every special day. On Leslie's and my junior high school graduation, my foster parents took us out to eat at a restaurant. Our high school graduations were a little more elaborate but when each one of us graduated from San Diego State University, Mr. and Mrs. Lorenzana felt so proud of us that a band was hired to provide some dance music and we were allowed to invite our friends. We really enjoyed those days. I always had a lot of fun at those events but on our last one I had more fun than my sisters did because that was when I met my prince charming," I bragged.

"Who was that prince charming you met?" Richard asked with a little tint of jealousy.

"Who else? You were, of course!" I answered. "Remember the time we had at our wedding a few months ago, thanks to my foster parents?" I asked.

"Yeah, it was great! And your whole family was great!" he answered. "I love you, sweetheart," he added.

"I love you, too, honey!" I said before he gave me a big, long kiss.

We immediately went to bed and my long nightmare was quickly forgotten. From then on, thanks to the happiness I have enjoyed with my husband and with my foster family, I simply hung on to the happy memories I have of my mother, my father, my stepfather and my grandparents

WAS IT HATE OR
WAS IT LOVE?

When I was fifteen years old, I had two high school classmates named Clara Layman and Johnny Sheridan. Clara was terribly afraid of spiders. We had a few discussions after school and, one day, when I asked her why she was afraid of spiders, she opened her heart to me.

Do you really want to know the secret why I get so jumpy over the sight of spiders?" she asked me.

"Sure! If you want to tell me, I'm all ears," I answered.

"Okay, but promise me you won't tell anyone about what I am going to tell you," she said. "Will you promise?" she begged.

"Yes, yes, I promise! It can't be so serious that I have to make a promise. Is it?" I asked.

"Well, to me it is very serious. If it weren't, I would not ask you for your word," she asserted.

"Okay, I give you my solemn promise. But I don't know why you trust me if it is so serious," I complained.

"When I talk to you, I get the impression that you are a very serious and honest person. That's why I feel I can trust you with my secret," she confessed.

"Thanks for your confidence in me but I don't think you should trust anyone with your secrets," I told her.

"I'm sure you can be trusted. Here it is," she offered. "I was not as jumpy before I met Johnny Sheridan. We were friends from the sixth grade up to until last year. We got along great. We became sweethearts three months after we met. He would walk me home after school and sometimes he would come visit me at my house where we would talk about a lot of things. One day, our discussion did not end too well," she confided.

"Who is your favorite singer?" he asked me.

"Elvis Presley, of course," I answered.

"Why him? What do you like about his singing?" Johnny wanted to know.

"I don't know. I think his movements when he's singing excite me," I confessed. Who is your favorite singer?" I asked him.

"I don't really have a favorite one. I like three of them: Perry Como, Dean Martin and Frank Sinatra," he answered.

"Why them? They hardly move when they're singing. To me that's boring," she stated.

"But they can really sing. Their voices are so smooth. That is why they are called crooners," Johnny defended them. "Elvis is not a real good singer. What makes him a favorite of the teenagers is his movement as he sings. They think it is sexy," he added. "Do you think he's sexy?" he asked.

"Yeah, I really think so," she purred. "Almost all my girlfriends think so, too," she added.

"What about your parents? Do they like him, too? Do they think he's sexy?" he asked.

"No, they don't and they don't want me to buy his records," she answered.

"Why not?" he asked.

"They say that his movements are dirty. But I like him anyway," she answered.

Clara went on to say that right then, Johnny began to sing a song and he did a few gyrations that upset her.

"Stop that, Johnny!" she screamed at him.

"Why don't you like me doing that? I think I can sing just as well as Elvis does!" he exclaimed.

"But your movements do look dirty!" she stated. "Don't do that again! Stick to your favorite singers' songs!" she begged.

"Okay, I will stop for now because I have to go home to do my homework," he stated.

"Yeah, go do your homework!" she insisted.

A few days later, Johnny walked Clara home and, again, they had a discussion that did not end too well.

"Today was report card day. Did you get yours, Clara?" Johnny asked.

"Yes, I did. It's inside my backpack," she answered.

"How was it? You must have done real well, right? Can you tell me the grades you got?" he asked

"Yes, I did okay but I don't want you to see it because it is too much trouble getting it out of my backpack," she answered.

"Here, I will take your report card out of your backpack," he offered.

"No, no, no! Show me yours first!" she insisted.

"Okay, here it is," he handed it to her.

Hey, three A's and three B's is not bad at all. Congratulations!" she said.

"But I did better than you!" she bragged.

"Well, if you did, why don't you want me to see your report card?" he asked.

"I told you! I have too many books in my backpack and it's too hard to get my report card out. Besides, we're in front of my house already and I have to go in. Sorry," she said.

Thus, Johnny never got to see Clara's first report card. She was probably embarrassed to show her grades. On the last day of school, Johnny walked Clara home and they began a conversation about the end of their eighth grade.

"Well, we are finally out of junior high school, Clara," Johnny said. "Do you realize that we are now freshmen in high school?" he asked.

"Yeah, isn't it great!" she answered. "And we are a year older," she added.

"Yes, we are!" he exclaimed. "Hey, you never showed me your first report card. Are you going to show me your last one?" he asked. "You have it in your hands. Now I have a chance to see your grades for both semesters. I want to see all your A's and B's," he added.

"Okay, I guess I don't have an excuse this time. Here it is. But don't make fun of my grades, okay?" she begged.

When Johnny saw the report card, he shouted. "Hey, you did get one A. Well, an A standing on one leg, one B, two C's and two D's. That gives you a D+ average. That is not a passing grade. Next semester don't lie about your grades. You know I get better grades than you. You did much better this last semester. You got an A, three B's and two C's. That's a strong C+ average. Who knows? Maybe next year you'll get better grades than I will. But if you don't study, you never will. I'm sorry I laughed at your grades. It won't happen again. I apologize. In fact, I will never ask you to show me your grades. I will wait for you to show them to me, if you want to do it," he promised.

After Johnny laughed at Clara's grades, she made it a point of not running into him. She had begun to dislike him and that dislike had become almost hate.

The next time she saw him was in high school. She saw him walking toward her and she tried to avoid him but she failed miserably. They came face to face, they said "hi" to each other and then he asked, "Are you still angry at me for laughing at your poor grades last year?"

"Well, I had planned not to talk to you anymore but I guess it's impossible since we both are attending the same high school. We are bound to bump into each other often. But I am still mad at you," she told him.

"I already apologized for laughing at your grades. Forgive me and let's continue being friends," he suggested.

"Well, okay, we'll still be friends. But you have to promise not to do anything that will embarrass and make me angry. Will you promise?" she begged.

"Yes, I promise and cross my heart," he answered.

For a long time I had known that they liked each other but Johnny was such a prankster that no promise was going to keep him from being the way he was. And sure enough, the next time he saw her walking ahead of him, he was playing with a daddy long leg spider in his hand and, right away, that gave him an idea. As he caught up with her, he dropped the spider on her hair as he shouted, "Clara, there's a spider on your hair!"

"EeeeeeeeK! Where? Get it off me, please! Hurry, hurry!!" she screamed.

She wildly flailed at her hair trying to knock the spider off, running back and forth at the same time until Johnny said, "I knocked it off already. Stop running! Look, it's only a daddy long leg. They are harmless," he told her.

"Oh, my God, was I scared! I told you I'm dreadfully afraid of spiders, all kinds of spiders. How could it have gotten on my hair"? It couldn't have been flying in the air! How did it get there?" she wanted to know.

"I don't know. Maybe you walked by a spider web or sat on the grass and it climbed onto your hair," he answered.

"Wait a minute! I didn't sit on the grass and I didn't walk by any spider web! You probably put it on my hair as you caught up with me! Didn't you?" she angrily asked.

"Okay, okay, I did it," he answered. "It was only a prank. I know they are harmless. Don't make such a big deal!" he added.

"You are terrible! You promised you would never do anything to embarrass me or make me angry and you have just done both things. You broke our promise. I won't trust you anymore. In fact, we are no longer friends. I hate you. Get away from me and stay as far away as you can!" she demanded.

"That was a cruel thing for him to do," I told Clara. "But that was some time back. How are you and he getting along now? Have you talked to each other lately?" I asked her.

"From that day on, we never spoke to each other again. I hate him with all my guts. And to think that I had begun to like him a lot. What I don't want you to tell anyone is that I am afraid of spiders and that I liked him. He made me look like a fool in front of many students. Please don't tell anyone, Pedro," she begged.

"I won't tell anyone," I promised.

I did not see either Johnny or Clara for eight long years until I went to a party held at one of my friend's house. They were both there and I was surprised they were very close to each other. They were actually hugging and kissing, which surprised me. I had to find out what had happened so I asked them right away,

"Hey, how come you two are so close together? I thought Clara hated you!"

"Well, she did tell me she hated me when we were in high school. But I didn't blame her. I was terrible to her, teasing her and frightening her with my spiders," Johnny answered.

"Well, I thought I did at that time but later I came to the realization that he did those things only to impress me. He confessed his sins to me when we coincidentally ended up taking a course in Zoology in college. By that time he had gotten rid of that awful habit of playing pranks on people. I was able to learn a lot about spiders and my strong fear of them vanished. It's not gone completely, mind you. I still try to stay away from the venomous ones." she explained.

"And you probably realized that you were really in love with each other, right?" I inquired. "I am so glad you are good friends now," I added.

"We are not good friends anymore!" she stated.

"She is right, Pedro," Johnny echoed.

"So how come you are so close together and kissing?" I asked.

"We are husband and wife now! We got married after we graduated from college," she proudly answered.

"My God, that's a big surprise to me! I'm so glad for you! Congratulations!

"Thank you very much, Pedro," they answered in unison.

We talked for a while and when it was time to leave our friend's house, we hugged and said our goodbyes to each other and I left thinking of how strange life is at times. A turbulent, almost love-hate relationship ended in deep love and matrimony. That was a happy ending, I must say!

THE STORY OF ROY, TOM AND JERRY

I am a teacher and this year my classroom is made up of eight-year olds. Most of my children are very well-behaved but I have two of them, Johnny and Pepe, who want to do practically whatever they want. I have used different methods in trying to teach them how to behave, especially to learn to follow instructions but I have had no success. Finally, I gathered them around me during story time and I told them, "Okay, children, today I'm going to tell you a story about a chubby little man named Roy and a chubby mouse named Jerry. I don't know how but they could understand each other and they both thought they were tough.

One day, Roy rented a room at a very cheap hotel. He did not want to spend too much money because he was kind of cheap. For some reason, the hotel owner allowed renters to bring their pets, as long as they were not big ones. Tom brought his beloved cat named Tom with him.

It so happens that some of the people staying at the hotel, including Roy, knew there was a mouse staying there, too. Since it never bothered them, they did not mind seeing it once in a while. In fact, they were so used to seeing it they named it Jerry.

Roy had seen Jerry often and he would curse him out loud every time he saw him, even though he knew the mouse wouldn't understand a word he was saying, so he thought. Jerry had lived in the hotel for so long, he had, somehow, learned to understand what the people were telling him every time they saw him. Jerry, of course, never talked back to them, but he could have if he had wanted to.

Roy had learned to hate the mouse so he decided to move to another room, hoping he would not see Jerry again. For a while, they did not run into each other but one day, Jerry was scurrying down a hall when he saw Roy coming toward him. As Roy came nearer, Jerry faced him and told him," I heard you moved into another room so you wouldn't have to see me again? Well, here we are face to face again and I have to tell you something about your new room."

"Ah, so you can talk, heh? How did you learn to do it? Never mind!" he said. "I have something to tell you first. You had better be careful. My cat has been looking for you and one of these days he is going to catch you. Tom plans to have you for dinner."

"Don't worry about me. I know how to defend myself. I've seen Jerry often and he doesn't look too smart. He has chased me several times but I'm too smart for him. He'll never catch me," Jerry bragged.

"Don't be too sure of yourself. Your luck may run out and Jerry will have you as his meal one of these days. Be on the lookout for him!" Roy said.

"I will," Jerry answered. "But listen, I will tell you about your new room. Many people have stayed there and never lasted more than one day. Do you know why? Of course you don't but I will tell you. I heard that everyone who has left that room went out scratching themselves, with welds all over their bodies. The beds in that room must be infested with something bad. I heard someone call them bed bugs. Why else would people leave that room scratching themselves so much? Don't be offended if I tell you to sleep with your clothes on. One bite is better than many bites. You are a little chubby and those bugs will leave you skinny after sucking all your blood," Jerry told Roy. "Do what I tell you and if you see me tomorrow, tell me how your night was," Jerry added.

Jerry giggled, said something else under his breath and, very sure of himself, scurried away as Roy turned around angrily, ignoring what Jerry had told him.

When night came, still angry, he took off all his clothes and went to bed.

When he got up the next morning, he felt very uncomfortable as his whole body was itching. When he went to the living room, he found his cat chubbier than the day before and he thought, "Well, I guess Tom finally made a good meal out of Jerry. I warned that poor mouse to be careful but I guess he did not listen to me. Ouch! Something must have pinched or bitten me last night. My whole body itches and I have scratches all over my body. Poor Jerry was right. The bed must be full of fat bed bugs after sucking all my blood. I should have done what he told me to do but I was so mad I forgot to sleep with my clothes on. Jerry must not have done what I told him and it cost him his life. Because I did not do what he told me to do, I am full of bites but, at least, I'm still alive. I had better stop being so cheap and go to a nicer hotel that is free of bed bugs. That was some night I spent at the cheap hotel. I think I have learned my lesson."

"Well, children, what do you think of Roy and Jerry? Do you think they should have followed each other's advice?" I asked the class.

"Yes!" they answered in unison.

"What about you, Pepe and Johnny? Do you think Roy and Jerry should have followed each other's advice?" I asked them.

"Yes, teacher, we both think so," Pepe and Johnny answered at the same time.

"Why do you think so? I asked.

"When you don't do what your teacher or your parents tell you to do, something bad happens to you," answered Johnny.

"Yes, that is always true. That's why we all should follow good advice. We would live a happier life if we obeyed and followed our teachers' and parents' advice all the time," I told them. "Okay, children, our story is over. Let's get ready to go out to recess," I told them. "Remember the story and what happened to Roy and Jerry because they did not follow each other's advice," I added.

From that day on, Pepe and Johnny behaved better. They still had bad days but not very often. I would say that the story left a good impression on them.

❖

CHILDHOOD ANECDOTES

Throughout my long life, I have seen and experienced many anecdotes that were amusing and darned right scary. Too bad my mind is not as sharp as when I was younger. If it were, I would recount many more than the few ones I will print here.

Attempted Kidnapping

At one time, just before we were to come to the U. S., four of us in the family were working in a farmland owned by Mr. Ramírez and my fifteen year old sister's job was to prepare and take our lunch to us. Mr. Ramírez's son, who was also working there, happened to be my sister's boyfriend. When lunch time came, he disappeared from sight and we wondered where he had gone.

Soon after, crying and looking scared, my sister arrived with our lunch. She told Mother that her boyfriend had met her at a spot not far from where we were, had gotten off his horse and had gotten into a conversation with her about her coming trip to America. She said he told her that he was not going to let her go to America. An argument ensued and, because he did not like what she told him, he tried to force her onto the horse, which was standing right next to her. Though she was afraid, she had the good sense to slap the horse on its rump. The horse took off running in the direction she had come from and he took off after it. That gave her a chance to hurry to our spot without any more dangerous incidents.

My mother complained to our boss, his father, and he gave this bold teenager a horrific scolding right in front of us when he appeared. For the rest of the week, she wouldn't dare go out of the house because she was afraid he would somehow try to keep her from making her trip to America.

The following Monday, we walked all three of them, Mother, Eva and Petra, to the train stop and they took off without a glitch. That was a relief and the incident remained etched in our minds for a long, long time.

Kissing a Corpse's Feet

When my father died, my mother and my grandmother did not know where to display his body so that visiting friends who came to pay their respects would view his body as they came into the house. There were two rooms with a door between them so they opted for putting his bed, with his body on it, right in front of the door.

There was a belief that if children were made to kiss the deceased person's feet, they would not be afraid to be near him afterward. Well, this is a completely erroneous belief as most children were afraid even after kissing their relatives' feet. All my siblings and I cried out loud as they forced us to kiss my dad's feet. It certainly did not work for me, specifically.

Hours after the kissing incident, I came back from outside and stood right at the door, facing my father's body. A white cloth had been placed over his face because he had died with his eyes open. When my aunt saw me standing on the door, knowing how brave I was, she took the cloth off his face and, suddenly, I could swear he was looking straight at me with his wide eyes. I let out a loud scream and dashed out of the house crying. They forced me to come back inside the house and they tried desperately to get me close to him but I cried so loudly and so much that they gave up and let me loose. I ran out of there as if the devil was chasing me and, for a long time, I remained afraid to come near a dead body.

Light by Lightning

My home village was a backward place in 1945: It was overgrown with bushes. There was no electricity. We could count on only one store. The store owner was probably the only one who owned a radio. There were no paved streets. TV's were unheard of.

When I was living there, it was, and still is, a place where rain comes down in buckets from June to September, almost every day and all of a sudden. One minute the sky is clear and the next minute a big storm makes its presence, with lightning flashing every few minutes. Most of the storms were scary for both adults and children, but especially for children. But night storms were the worst. I remember being sent to the store, a few blocks away, to buy some drastically needed groceries and it was a terrifying ordeal. I saw myself navigating gallantly, walking down the streets only a short distance at a time. You see, I had to wait for lightning to strike so I could see what was ahead of me before I continued to walk. Always waiting for flashes of lightning to light up my way was the routine followed. As you can guess, a trip to the store at night took a long time and it was a scary adventure, especially for children.

Domestic cows are always freely roaming the streets. They were always looking for something to eat, like grass on the streets or bushes on the side of the street. When the storms hit early in the evening and the sky was covered with dark clouds, these cows, standing or laying down, posed a great danger for whoever was walking down the streets. I happened to run into one or two cows often when I went to the store during a storm. Fortunately, cows did not have horns so one simply ran into them with no major consequences.

Another thing that made walking on the streets at night a nightmare were the stories about ghosts. We always heard parents tell us, "Beware, for a lady wearing a long white robe appears here and there!" "That house over there is haunted so try to avoid walking near it." "If you hear an owl hooting on top of a house, it means that someone died there and that owl happens to be her/his spirit."

This was a very lawless area and killings were very common. What made this matter worse for children was that every spot where a person was killed, his or her ghost was supposed to appear and parents kept reminding us about these apparitions.

As I grew into a man, I realized that we, as children, were afraid of anything because our parents told us so many stories about ghosts in attempts to get us to comply with their rules. They wanted obedient little children and that was about the only way they got what they wanted. I remember my mother telling us, "If you don't obey and do what I tell you, the ground will open up and eat you!" or "If you keep being a bad boy, the devil will take you with him!"

Superstition was prevalent then, especially among the poor, uneducated citizens. Now I watch images of my village on TV showing that electricity has arrived, people dress as modernly as in nearby Mexicali and here, streets are paved, cows are kept in corrals, one third of the inhabitants own TVs and radios, and most of the people have at least a six grade education. All these modern conveniences tell me that superstition has almost disappeared.

Swearing Has Consequences

My oldest sister had a boyfriend whom Mother loved maybe more than my sister did and whom I hated. I was only ten years old and I happened to be working at the same farm field where he was. He, being much older than I, was holding the plow as a pair of oxen was pulling it to open the ground. I was following behind dropping corn seeds and covering them with my feet.

During lunch time, another worker and I were away from the fire where the others were heating their lunches. He and others knew I disliked my sister's boyfriend and they liked to tease me about it. We were sitting down eating our lunches when he said, "Hey, Julian, your brother-in-law says that you are his favorite brother-in-law."

"Tell him to go to hell!" I answered. I said something else worse but I cannot repeat it right now. Well, when I got home, my mother called me on it.

"Why did you tell Jose to go to hell? Why are you hurling all kinds of expletives at him just because someone told you he was your brother-in-law?"

"I didn't tell him anything! I told someone else to tell him that because they kept on teasing me! And why do you defend him so vehemently? He's not your boyfriend! He's Eva's boyfriend, not her husband!" I replied angrily.

She quickly grabbed a whip that lay on a bench nearby, wheeled around and hit me with it on my upper arm, opening a gash that began to bleed. It hurt so much I started to cry and ran out of the house toward my godfather's house in the next block.

I was so angry at her for what I thought was an unfair whipping that I stayed with my godfather for three weeks. I worked with him at his fields, ate and slept in his house. I missed my siblings but I was happy where I was. I would have stayed there longer had not my mother convinced me to come back home.

Three weeks later, my godfather went to the store and he took me with him. The owner was his close friend so he went inside and I sat on a bench outside. After a few minutes, I took a glance toward one side of the street and I spotted my mother coming toward me. I waited there and she sat down with me. She asked me how I was and I said I was okay. She apologized to me and asked me, "Are you ever going to come back home, son? We miss you."

"I don't want to go back!" I answered. "I am happy living and working with my godfather. Why do you want me back, so you can beat the hell out of me again? No thanks!" I answered.

I did miss my family but at that moment I was really angry at her. After a long silence, she used good strategy as she began to cry and said, "Your dad has just left us and now you want to leave us too. Please come back, son. We all miss you. I promise I will never lay a hand on you. I know now I shouldn't have done it. I'm sorry."

I would have stayed at my godfather's had not my mother convinced me to come back home. I felt so sorry for her I began to cry with her and I agreed to return home with her.

I went inside to talk to my godfather and told him about my decision. He told me he had enjoyed my stay with him and that it was okay because I was doing the right thing. I thanked him for putting up with me and I left, hoping my mom would keep her promise not to whip me again. From then on until she died, she never again laid a hand on me angrily, thank God!

Beware of La Llorona

In my home village, there were very few means of entertainment for children in 1945. A favorite one was the gathering of anywhere from five to ten boys behind a certain house to shoot the breeze. These gatherings usually ended well with the children returning to their houses with new stories or anecdotes weaned from each other. But one specific gathering remained in my mind for quite a long time.

Near my house lived four or five friends who often came together after finishing their school homework. We usually met behind my house and joked around playing pranks on each other or exchanging stories or gossip. These gatherings would sometimes last for hours into the night, sometimes ending in frightful situations.

One day, Mario, Jose, Enrique, Juan, Pedro and I decided to meet behind my house to have fun sharing stories. Most of the stories included some of the stories told to us by our own family members. Spooky stories were allowed only during daylight hours and were taboo after sunset hours, for obvious reasons.

At one of our gatherings, one day, the story being told at the time was so interesting we forgot all about our taboo rule. We had no idea what time it was as watches were unheard of among us then. The only thing that made us aware of the darkness that had fallen was the story Jose was telling about the Llorona. This story tells about a lady who had killed her children and, upon her death, was cursed to wander in the world searching for her lost children. According to legend, as she walks searching for them, she lets out a long, sad, wailing cry calling their names. When we realized what the story was about, we tried desperately to stop his narration, especially when we all heard his imitation of her wailing cry, "Toñoooooooooooooooh! Linaaaaaaaaah!"

"Shut up, Jose! Don't do that!" Juan interrupted.

"Yes, Jose, don't do that! Stop your story, please!" Pedro begged.

"What? I'm not doing that! Enrique must have done it. I stopped talking a few minutes ago, just as I heard the wailing!" Jose explained.

"You did not do the wailing sound, Jose? You're the one telling the story so we thought you had done it. Who did then?" Mario asked.

"I don't know!" Jose replied. "I heard it myself far away! That was why I stopped my narration!" he exclaimed.

The wailing sound was heard again and this time it sounded closer. We all turned toward the sound and what we saw froze us momentarily. It looked like a lady dressed in white, walking very slowly toward us. As she wailed, she raised her arms toward the sky as if pleading to God to return her children to her.

As we regained our composure, we all wanted to run home but we did not dare. Instead, we started talking to each other.

"Jose, walk me home, please! I live the farthest and I'm afraid to go by myself!" Enrique begged.

"Are you crazy? I live just as far away as you do and this lady seems to be right in front of my house! I can't walk you home! You walk me home!" Jose answered

"Pedro and Juan, you and I live close to each other on the other end of the street! Let's run home together before the lady comes closer to us!" Mario said.

"Okay, let's go!" Pedro agreed.

Jose lived right across my house so he, too, took off when Pedro, Mario and Juan left.

They took off leaving Enrique and me to face La Llorona. We were behind my house so I could have just run inside but I did not want to leave Enrique alone. He and I remained huddled together, scared to death.

We watched the wailing lady getting closer and closer to where we were but now she seemed to be floating about two feet off the ground.

As the lady in white was about to cross in front of us, I began to scream at the top of my lungs, "Mother! Mother! Come outside, mother!

The lady in white seemed to turn to face us as my mother asked, "What's the matter? Why are you screaming so loudly?"

"We saw the Llorona coming toward us! She was walking very slowly, crying out for her children. We weren't too scared until she got close to us!" Enrique exclaimed.

"There is no such thing as La Llorona! You've heard so many stories about her you're beginning to believe it. You boys were probably talking about ghosts so when someone went walking by, you thought it was a ghost." Mother said.

"No, Mrs. Loreto. We all saw her and she was crying loudly, "Toñooooooooooooh! Linaaaaaaaaaaah! Toñooooooooooooh! Linaaaaaaaaaaah! Before she got close to us, Juan, José, Pedro and Mario ran home. I did not run home because my house is on the end of the street where she was coming from. I was afraid to meet her on the way!" Enrique argued.

"Where is she then? I did not see her!" my mother complained. "You just imagined it. You shouldn't talk about spooky things when you get together, especially at night!" she advised us.

"You did not see her because when you asked 'What's the matter?' she disappeared!" I exclaimed.

"Okay, okay! Let's take Enrique home because it's kind of late and both of you have to go to sleep. And don't forget, there's no such thing as ghosts. They're just the product of people's imagination," my mother said.

"Okay, Mrs. Loreto, whatever you say. I am so happy you came out when your son called you. Thank you for saving us from La Llorona!" Enrique said.

SIMPLE POEMS
FOR EVERYONE

AMATEUR POET

I'm an amateur and I do not have an inkling
As to what poem writing is really about.
But deep in my mind I can't but keep on thinking,
That I'll do it, no matter what will come out.

I assure you, what I write will be quite simple,
And I know that the reader will criticize.
He will smile and that way will show a dimple,
Thinking that, for sale, my poems will have no price.

It's okay because they are not up for sale.
I just want the reader to know what I feel.
If I planned to sell them, I know I would fail.
And taking money for them would be a steal.

So just read them for the sake of simply reading,
And I promise that someday good poems I'll write.
But I hope that many readers will be seething,
With desire to read my poems day and night.

I had better start on that important trek,
So, for now, my good-byes to all I will send.
I pray that on my way I will have no wreck,
So that idle a long time I will not spend.

Many of my poems in English will be written.
Many others in Spanish I will engage.
Some readers will with the English bug be bitten,
While others in Spanish will read page by page.

MY BIRTHDAY IS COMING

MY BIRTHDAY IS COMING
AND I'M KIND OF SAD
IT'S KIND OF ALARMING
'CAUSE I'M KIND OF MAD

I WILL HAVE TO WAIT
TO SEE WHAT THEY DO
A GIFT WOULD BE GREAT
A HUG WILL BE, TOO

NOTHING I'VE BEEN TOLD
AS THE DAY APPROACHES
EVERYBODY IS SO COLD
AND THAT COLD ENCROACHES

BUT NOW THAT I'M OLD
A HUG WILL SUFFICE
FOR SPENDING THE GOLD
IS A GREAT SACRIFICE

THEY ARE ALL SO MUM
NOT A WORD THEY'RE SAYING
NOT EVEN A HUM
IN RESPECT THEY'RE PAYING

THAT I'M EIGHTY-THREE
I DON'T WANT TO SHOUT
I DON'T WANT TO BE
ABOUT MY AGE PROUD

I WOULD RATHER HEAR
IN MY EAR THE RINGING,
'CAUSE THE DAY'S SO NEAR,
SOMEONE'S HAPPY SINGING

I'VE LIVED LONG ENOUGH
AND LIVED WITH GREAT PASSION
BUT LIFE HAS BEEN TOUGH
PLEASE, GOD, HAVE COMPASSION

FOR THEN I WOULD KNOW
THAT THEY ARE AWARE
AND THAT WAY THEY'LL SHOW
THAT FOR ME THEY CARE

IF I LIVE MUCH LONGER
GIVE ME YOUR PROTECTION
AND MAKE ME MUCH STRONGER
AND FILLED WITH ELATION

I'M ALMOST EIGHTY-TWO

I'M ALMOST EIGHTY-TWO
AND I FEEL PRETTY OLD
THERE IS A LOT TO DO
TO DO THEM IS MY GOAL

I KNOW IT WILL BE HARD
FOR I AM GETTING WEAK
I KNOW I HAVE TO START
THOUGH I'VE A YELLOW STREAK

I AM AFRAID TO FAIL
IN THIS GIGANTIC TASK
I'M OLD AND I'M QUITE FRAIL
IT'S JUST TOO MUCH TO ASK

A FAILURE IN CAREGIVING
AS WELL AS IN COMPOSING
I HOPE YOU'LL BE FORGIVING
THAT ON THE JOB I'M DOZING

EFFORT IS NEVER LACKING
TIME IS WHAT IS SO FLEETING
MY BRAIN I'M ALWAYS WRACKING
MORE TIME IS WHAT I'M NEEDING

NOT MY SONGS NOR MY SINGING
WILL BRING ME ANY WEALTH
ALL THEY WILL END UP BRINGING
IS NOTHING BUT ILL HEALTH

BUT I WILL KEEP ON WRITING
PERHAPS I WON'T SUCCEED
BUT IT IS SO EXCITING
A GREAT HOBBY, INDEED

IF FAILURE IN THIS ATTEMPT
COMES AS PER ALL THE ODDS
I'M SURE I'LL FEEL CONTEMPT
THAT WILL IS SURELY GOD'S

CREATOR, AFTER ALL,
AND I'LL ACCEPT HIS WILL
IN THIS PERHAPS I'LL FALL
BUT I HAVE ONE CARD STILL

I HAVE MY SINGING VOICE
AND CHURCH IS WHERE I'LL SING
HE'S GIVING ME THAT CHOICE
MY VOICE TO HIM I'LL BRING

RESULTS ARE ALWAYS LATE
'CAUSE TIME KEEPS SPEEDING BY
AND COMING IS THE DATE
WHEN I WILL SAY GOOD-BYE

MY SINGING JOB'S A BUST
COMPOSING HAS NO END
BUT DOING THE BEST I MUST
UNTIL MY WILL WILL BEND

IF EVERY HARD ENDEAVOR
WILL CAUSE YOU GREAT DISPLEASURE
TAKE ME, DO ME THE FAVOR
I'LL GO WITH YOU WITH PLEASURE

IT'S TIME TO GO ANYWAY
I HAVE BEEN HERE TOO LONG
I SHOULD BE ON MY WAY
YOU'LL SOON TAKE ME ALONG

WHILE I HAVE ALL MY WITS
I HOPE I'LL GET YOUR CALL
BEFORE, IN LITTLE BITS,
ALL ONE BY ONE THEY'LL FALL

I'M EIGHTY-ONE YEARS OLD
AND SOON I WILL BE GONE
MY VOICE IS GOOD, I'M TOLD
THAT IS WRITTEN IN STONE

IF ALL IS TO NO AVAIL
OF TRYING I WILL BE TIRED
IF IN THIS I WILL FAIL
MY VOICE WILL BE RETIRED

THAT WAY I WILL BE CERTAIN
NOT RIDDEN IN BED I'LL BE
IN THEIR EYES A GREAT BURDEN
IN ME THEY WILL NOT SEE

BUT I WILL ALONG TREAD
AS LONG AS I'M ALIVE
WISHING FOR, INSTEAD,
A CURE FOR MY SICK WIFE

I MERELY WANT A BREAK
FROM ALL I HAVE GONE THROUGH
WOULD IT NOT BE JUST GREAT
TO GET WHAT ONE IS DUE?

LONG AGE WEARS AND TEARS

Real skills I really didn't have many
But I must say that I had a few
It's better than not having any
Because then you have nothing to do

We all sooner or later find out
That long age brings wears, tears and some more
And that we simply can't live without
All those great things we could do before

I could walk, run, jump and even dance
Obstacles were to me really unknown
I always used them at every chance
And doing them well I always have shown

My lovemaking my wife really enjoyed
When I sang she was quite overjoyed
Now those same skills I try to avoid
Because they seem to get her annoyed

One of those skills has just disappeared
'Cause she can't concentrate anymore
Away from those same acts we have steered
Because she thinks they are just a bore

Now my singing's in hibernation
Because now to nobody I can sing
There's no end to my deep frustration
And I'm sure I can't do anything

As far as basketball and dancing
I do not anymore try to attempt
When at people doing them I'm glancing
For those people I feel great contempt

Though in my writing and my singing
My caregiving has greatly interfered
With those skills I will keep on swinging
Now that those others have disappeared

When you reach a definitive age
Many things really accumulate
Gray hair and wrinkles become the rage
Aches and pains come with many birthdates

Then we find out we no more can do
The things we could do so long ago
And then we begin to realize, too
That some more of our skills will soon go

I AM FEELING LOW

I DON'T KNOW WHAT'S WRONG WITH ME
I KNOW I AM FEELING LIKE HELL
I WONDER WHAT IT COULD BE
BUT I WISH I WAS FEELING WELL

A GOOD DOCTOR I WILL PICK
HE WILL BE THE ONE WHO WILL KNOW
FOR SURE IF I COULD BE SICK
AND WHY I HAVE BEEN FEELING LOW

I CANNOT DO VERY MUCH
NOW THAT I HAVE LOST MY REAL MUSE
HER BODY'S HEALTH IS SUCH
THAT MUCH OF IT SHE CANNOT USE

SO CHEERFUL AND FULL OF LIFE
THAT SHE HAD KEPT ME ON MY FEET
SHE WAS SUCH AN ACTIVE WIFE
ALWAYS KEEPING ME OFF MY SEAT

'DO THIS, DO THAT, MY LOVE'
INCITING ME ON TO ACTION
IT WAS NEVER REALLY TOUGH
TO KEEP AWAY FROM INACTION

WHATEVER GOALS I HAVE MET
I CAN SAY THAT SHE WAS BEHIND
IF SOME GOALS I FAILED TO GET
THE REAL REASONS SHE HELPED ME FIND

WHEN NEW GOALS TO SET I TRY
SHE TENDS TO URGE ME ON AND ON
"AWAY DO NOT LET THIS FLY
IF YOU RELAX, IT WILL BE GONE"

ACHIEVEMENTS HAVE COME TO ME
SIMPLY BECAUSE SHE IS MY MUSE
BUT FROM NOW ON THAT CAN'T BE
BECAUSE HER I CAN NO MORE USE

INDIFFERENT TO ALL SHE IS
FOR NOW SHE CANNOT THINK OR TALK
MY INSPIRATION I WILL MISS
FOR NOW SHE CANNOT EVEN WALK

THE FEELING I HAD BEFORE
MAKES ME THINK THAT I'M JUST DEPRESSED
THERE WON'T BE WINS ANYMORE
FOR NOW NO ONE WILL BE IMPRESSED

NO NEW GOALS I WILL NOW PICK
AS I HAD BEEN DOING BEFORE
BUT I WILL BE FEELING SICK
FOR ACCLAIMS THERE WILL BE NO MORE

I WILL NOW JUST SIT BESIDE
MY MUSE, WHO IS NOW REALLY ILL
HER ILLNESS MY LIFE WILL GUIDE
SIMPLY WAITING FOR OUR LORD'S WILL

I HAD A DREAM

Last night I had a dream that was scary.
It was only a dream but I took it to heart.
It was quite vivid and left me weary.
I tried to get out of it but it was really hard.

Now, I am worried it just may come true.
I'm old and an omen it may very well be.
I'm okay now but I'm feeling quite blue.
A dream only but it may happen to me.

A teacher in limbo in my dream I was,
Lost in the woods and couldn't find my school.
Found on the road, anxiously waiting for a bus.
If a bus had come, it would have been cool.

I walked and I waited and no bus came by.
A teacher lost, I must have looked like a fool.
I walked and I found a little house nearby.
To people there I asked, "Where is my school?

With vacant eyes, they all looked at me.
They gave me direction and there I went.
I walked to the spot but nothing I could see
I did find that to the wrong place I had been sent.

I found myself nowhere and soon I realized,
That it was a dream, but what did it mean?
The feeling it left me with I really despised.
Will I really become the man in the dream?

Alzheimer's disease soon came to my head
Was my dream an omen of what I will be?
Will I be lost in the woods in the days ahead?
I really hope and pray that doesn't happen to me.

Having two dementia patients in a family,
A double burden it surely would be.
That burden in my family I would hate to see.
Please, God, don't let that happen to me!

I'm old and, at times, some things I forget.
But I'm hoping that it is because I am old.
"I'm sure that disease you never will get.
You still look too sharp!" I've been told.

When they tell me that, I knock on wood,
And hope that the Lord is always with me.
Forget that awful dream, I think I should,
And think that free of that disease I will be.

I WILL BE IN HEAVEN

The day is almost here
It is only a week away
In fact, it's very near
Way too close, if I may say

After that fateful day
All my worries will be gone
The hurting will go away
If the work is quite well done

Limping will disappear
And I will be walking tall
I will walk in high gear
To whatever is my call

After that fateful day
Many places I'll explore
Then I can really say
That I'm not slow anymore

I will be more alive
Much more than the last few years
For my life will be rife
With pleasures and without fears

Not a thing will stop me
From doing whatever I please
I will be where I will be
Always doing my thing with ease

I'll be happy up there
Rejoicing in His presence
Or I'll be happy here
Being mindful of His essence

Happy my love will be
To know that I am quite sound
Happy that my good knee
Will let me move her around

I will thank my dear Lord
If in heaven I end up
If I survive the sword
With cheers I will fill my cup

Heaven may be up high
Or it may be right down here
Either way, I will sigh
My relief will be sincere

She'll know I'll do her will
Whatever that requires
She'll know I always will
Give her what she desires

Then, nothing will stop me
My knee will be in top form
Quite ready I will be
Any hard task to perform

I'VE LOST ALL MY SKILLS

I've lost all my skills
They've all said good-bye
And with them the thrills
They used to provide

The gifts that my God
Was good to give me
I guess I forgot
Or they ceased to be

My good thinking cap
Has just gone astray
And that's a bum rap
Oh, why didn't it stay

Just where it has strayed
Is way beyond me
I wish it had stayed
Oh, where can it be

My legs always fail
Can't run anymore
They constantly ail
And they're always sore

My singing's okay
I can proudly say
I'll use it in May
My sweetheart's birthday

Often from my mind
That skill disappears
But I'm sure I'll find
It good for some years

But singing for me
Alone is no use
That singing can be
A real poor excuse

It's always been great
Singing to a crowd
For more is at stake
That would make me proud

But free time is gone
Always on my feet
My singing is done
I'll admit defeat

I go to the store
And come back in pain
Can't dance anymore
All effort's in vain

There's only one way
I will become free
By going away
Free from work I'll be

But only with God
I would like to live
For if not, I've got
More of me to give

If that's not to be
I cannot complain
I'll just wait and see
What He will ordain

I'll carry my pain
As well as I can
If He that ordains
I'll act like a man

Care giving's a must
I'm always tired
My tail I bust
Can't be retired

I will not complain
And I will not cry
I'll hide all my pain
My eyes will be dry

I am almost sure
That I will get by
But stress will ensure
That I will soon die

Quite happy I'll be
What a glorious day
My God I will see
I sure hope I may

BEING REALISTIC

I HAVE BEEN TOLD I'M PESSIMISTIC
IN ALL MY THINKING AND MY WRITING
I SIMPLY CAN'T BE OPTIMISTIC
WHEN MY HEALTH SIMPLY KEEPS ON SLIDING

I'M THINKING OF THE LAWS OF NATURE
OF MY BIRTH AND OF THE END OF LIFE
OF COURSE, I STILL CAN OFTEN CAPTURE
THE GRAND DELIGHT OF STILL BEING ALIVE

BUT I AM SIMPLY BEING REALISTIC
WHEN I DECLARE THAT I WILL SOON DIE
AT EIGHTY-THREE WHO'S OPTIMISTIC
IN THINKING THAT DEATH WILL PASS HIM BY

I WILL SURELY LET LIFE TAKE ITS COURSE
AND ENJOY IT FOR ALL THAT IT'S WORTH
WHAT'S LEFT OF IT I'LL ENJOY, OF COURSE
BECAUSE I KNOW GOD HAS THE LAST WORD

IN THE MEANTIME, I CANNOT BUT THINK
THAT MY LIFE IS COMING TO ITS END
PERHAPS I'M STILL NOT AT THE BRINK
BUT I HAVE TO THINK I'M AT THE BEND

AS SOON AS I LEAVE THAT BENDING CURVE
I WILL BE MEETING MY LORD ABOVE
AND AFTER MY LONG LIFE, I DESERVE
TO BE WITH MY LORD, THE KING OF LOVE

MY PESSIMISM WILL BE IN THE PAST
FOR HAPPY I'LL BE ETERNALLY
ANY SUFFERING AWAY I'LL CAST
AS GOD BY MY SIDE WILL ALWAYS BE

JOYFUL MY NEW LIFE I WILL NOW SEE
AS MY EARTHLY PROBLEMS ARE NO MORE
PESSIMISTIC NO MORE, FOR I'LL BE
OPTIMISTIC AS NEVER BEFORE

A TRIP WITH NO RETURN

A trip I am taking
From which I won't come back
It's not of my making
But I'm ready to pack

That trip I cannot stall
For it's taken by all
We all obey that call
Old, young or even small

I may go to a space
Where good cheer has no bounds
They say it is a place
Where happiness abounds

Have you paid a good price
A lot of people ask
Earning this paradise
Becomes a mighty task

If while you are alive
God's rules you never miss
I'm sure you'll earn that life
Of happiness and bliss

There is another place
Where my long trip may end
A real hot desert space
Where all my time I'll spend

There is never relief
For cool you'll never be
Where you will always beef
For rain you'll never see

Will I be ending there
And burn eternally
Have I been good or fair
Or bad I've been really

I will tell you one thing
I truly have to say
That of the rules I think
Those rules I should obey

Are these sites really there
Some say that that's a myth
I hope it won't be where
The rest of me will sit

Has someone seen that place
And come right back to tell
Has he come face to face
With it for years to dwell

They say our trip will end
At a hole near our homes
Where worms will surely spend
Eating even our bones

A good or a bad being
We'll be there anyway
Worms may eat everything
We won't feel it, they say

I'm ready to embark
I'm almost on my way
Just where I'll disembark
I really cannot say

But I sure hope and pray
That wherever I stay
I can come back to say
That if you're good, it'll pay

I won't discuss the place
The place where I reside
'Cause I want to save face
For it will hurt my pride

NOW IT'S YOUR TURN

Now that we're old, we're just like little babies.
We cannot do some things that we could do when young.
We recall that years ago, you had these same problems.
Your legs didn't seem to work and you couldn't eat by yourselves,
But you never worried because you had lots of help.
We put you in our arms and took you here and there.
And when you got real hungry, we served you baby food.
And with a little spoon, we put it in your mouth
Once a little older, you didn't need us as much.
When we served you your food, you ate it by yourselves.
And when the need arrived for you to empty yourselves,
We were always ready to wash your soiled diapers.
And when a little older, we'd take you to the bathroom.
There, you always took care of your needs by yourselves.
When babies, you got sick and to doctors we took you,
Or home remedies we would always provide you with.
Our roles have changed and now we are like two new babies
God has now taken away all those youthful abilities.
That's why we need for you to lend us your assistance.
We cannot walk too well and we cannot think clearly.
Our legs will not obey messages from our brains,
As the messages it sends, on their way get lost.
Our eyes, legs and hands are unable to decipher them.
Our speech is all garbled and we have lost our hearing,
So now it's your turn to take us here and there.
You must speak to us louder and listen more attentively.
We soon will disappear and no more we will bother you.
You will not have to worry, for you will not be burdened,
With taking us to there or bringing us right back.
You will not have to shout so we can understand,

Nor pay real close attention to understand our speech.
But don't leave us alone while we are still around,
Even if we're senile and everything is wrong.
Maybe it is your work, or maybe it's the distance,
Or perhaps your families don't allow you to visit us.
We can't believe it's lack of love or lack of interest,
That keeps you all away and makes you not to care.
We don't know what it is, but we'll leave it all to God!

A GREAT LOVE AFFAIR

Quite a few years ago,
   we heard of many a fight
   that happened every night.
Ill feelings there were so.
   The west was always west.
   The east was always east.
One side was called the beast
   and that side was aware
   but it didn't really care.

Our children went to school
   at their own neighborhood.
The west thought it was cool.
   The other side didn't care
Bad blood was everywhere.
With tension in the air,
   something had to be done
   before fist-fighting would
   turn to fights with a gun.

Morale is really okay.
   The children are the best.
The rules they do obey
   in their great learning quest.
If some get out of hand
   and overstep their bounds,
   those children our boss hounds.
Virtues of rules he expounds.
   Compliance he'll demand.

The children do regret
   behaving like great fools.
But children do forget
   the purpose for these rules.
They know that in societies
   where all do as they please,
   people don't feel at ease
   because there is no peace.
They're not democracies.

Our district a plan set
    where children from both sides
    would go to different schools.
The idea was a good bet.
Some children took bus rides
    that became daily pools.
Teachers were also involved
    and this de-neighborhood
    has been working real good.

Quite sorry we will be
    in three, two or one year,
    if we all live to see
    what we all seem to fear.
I'm sure we'll all bemoan,
    and even be in pain,
    if we don't see again
    all the great social gain
    the children all have shown.

Now children get along
    much better than before.
We hope this lasts for long
    and fights occur no more.
Some want a melting pot
    where we all live as one.
But as long as our Juan
    is kept away from John,
    this idea is going to pot

It seems as if we still
    have people who of late
    have not yet had their fill
    of racism and hate.
They're willing to erase
    all that children have done.
They want to take the fun
    and the peace they have won
    by living as one race.

Every teacher is great!
    We really get along!
This rapport will not break.
    It will remain for long.
It's not an endless love
    for each other we share.
But we don't really care,
    as long as this affair
    is blessed by God above.

We work as a good team:
    boss, teacher and the aide.
At times, it really seems
    that our smiles never fade
With our hearts full of glee,
    we do all things with zest.
I think we are the best
    of all the staffs in the West.
We're like a family.

The teachers at this school
　　their jobs they do enjoy.
Their work they think is cool
　　as it brings them great joy.
Their knowledge they impart
　　before their children leave.
You had better believe
　　that what children receive
　　comes from deep in the heart.

We think it's only fair
　　that our boss gets involved
　　in a problem we all share
　　that needs to be resolved.
I think we all will have
　　to wish, to hope and pray
　　that all of us will stay.
Who will be going away,
　　to break up our great staff?

One of the greatest guys
　　our boss, he really is.
With his wide-open eyes,
　　there's nothing he will miss.
To better our work do,
　　this way he helps us all.
But we must stand quite tall
　　if he should ever call,
　　or he'll bid us adieu.

Let's hope and pray, my friend,
　　that the children stay put.
But if the district sends
　　them to their neighborhood,
　　away peace they'll have thrown.
Let none of us forget
　　that this they'll soon regret.
For surely they will get
　　what they alone have sown.

LONG LIVE THE
GREATEST COUNTRY

OH, HOW BEAUTIFUL THIS COUNTRY
THAT HAPPENS TO BE MY HOME
OF THE COUNTRIES IN THE WORLD, IT
STANDS AT THE TOP ALONE
IN BEAUTY IT MAY HAVE EQUALS IN
TREASURES AND MANY MORE
BUT IN USING THESE RESOURCES THEY ARE STILL VERY POOR

ITS PEOPLE SO ENERGETIC AND RESOURCEFUL THEY HAVE BEEN
THEY HAVE WORKED TO MAKE THIS COUNTRY
THE BEST ANY ONE HAS SEEN
THEY HAVE THOUGHT OUT SOME IDEAS
THAT HAVE HURLED US TO THE TOP
THUS LURING THE RICH, THE HUMBLE
TO OUR LAND TO PUT UP SHOP

OPPORTUNITIES AND FREEDOMS
ATTRACT PEOPLE TO OUR LAND
WHERE WITH EFFORT AND PERSISTENCE
EVERYBODY CAN SUCCEED
I KNOW THAT WHEN THEIR NEW LANGUAGE
THEY SPEAK, WRITE AND UNDERSTAND
A NEW LIFE WITH OUR FREEDOMS, THEY
WILL SOON OBTAIN, INDEED

WE GIVE THANKS TO ALL THOSE HEROES
WHO ESTABLISHED OUR NEW LAND
THOSE WHO FOUGHT AGAINST THE BRITISH,
HUNGRY FOR A FREE COUNTRY
THOSE WHO WROTE OUR CONSTITUTION
PUTTING FREEDOMS IN OUR HANDS
AND ALL THE BRAVE MEN AND WOMEN WHO
HAVE FOUGHT TO KEEP US FREE

IT IS UP TO US THE LIVING TO OUR FREEDOMS GUARANTEE
BY SAFEKEEPING, BY ALL MEANS, AGAINST ALL OUR ENEMIES
BY GIVING OUR LIVES, IF NEED BE, THINKING OF POSTERITY
ONLY THAT WAY OUR GREAT COUNTRY
FOREVER GREAT IT WILL BE

AMERICA IS THE GREATEST, IS THE GREATEST IN THE WORLD
FOR IT OFFERS ALL ITS PEOPLE THE BEST LIFE THEY CAN GAIN
FOR THAT REASON VERY PROUDLY OUR
FLAG WILL BE UNFURLED
AND "LONG LIVE OUR GREATEST COUNTRY"
WILL ALWAYS BE MY REFRAIN

WHO AM I

For years confusion reigned,
   Quite deep inside my mind.
But answers never rained,
   And I'm still in a bind.

Our ancestors, I'm sure,
   Were Mexicans by birth.
And our line is still pure,
   But we don't now its worth.

Forever people called
   Us "dirty Mexicanos".
And we were quite appalled'
   For we're Americanos

Most teachers got upset
   When Spanish we would speak.
But we would never fret,
   For we were very meek.

Spanish was not allowed,
   Although our English stunk.
But we've always been proud
   Of our chicano spunk.

Our lives had gone quite sour.
   We could not see the light.
So we fought for Brown power.
   And now our path looks bright.

"Chicano" is certainly in,
   Although I still must find
A satisfactory "Fin"
   To troubles in my mind.

"Chicano" I do not like!
   I am a mexicano!
But I will go on strike
   And call myself mexico-americano

AMERICA IS MY COUNTRY

TO THIS AMAZING COUNTRY, LAND OF
THE FREE AND THE BRAVE
I CAME WHEN I WAS LITTLE, A BETTER LIFE TO FIND
FROM POVERTY AND TYRANTS I FINALLY FEEL SAFE
GOD AND MY EFFORTS HELPED ME LEAVE MY OLD LIFE BEHIND

IT WELCOMES ALL THE PEOPLE WHO
FOR THEIR FREEDOM YEARN
AND MANY, MANY OTHERS WHO HAVE LITTLE TO EAT
AS SOON AS HERE WE SETTLE, WE HAVE A CHANCE TO LEARN
THAT WITH A MIGHTY EFFORT, LIFE HERE WILL BE A TREAT

AMERICA, AMERICA, I'M PROUD TO CALL YOU HOME
AMERICA, AMERICA, THE PLACE I CALL MY OWN
I'M FROM A FOREIGN COUNTRY BUT HERE IS WHERE I'VE GROWN
AMERICA IS THE COUNTRY WHERE MY ROOTS I HAVE SOWN

AS SOON AS WE ARE ABLE, ITS VASTNESS WE CAN SEE
ITS BEAUTY AND ITS BOUNTY FROM SEA TO SHINING SEA
SEEING ALL THESE BOUNDLESS TREASURES,
WE SOON ARE MADE AWARE
THAT WE CAN CALL THEM OURS, FOR ALL OF THEM WE SHARE

AMERICAN, THEY CALL ME AND I FEEL VERY PROUD
BEING A SON OF THIS COUNTRY MAKES ME STAND VERY TALL
THANKFUL FOR ALL ITS BOUNTY, I FEEL THE NEED TO SHOUT
"LONG LIVE THE GREATEST COUNTRY AND MAY IT NEVER FALL!"

AMERICA, AMERICA, I'M PROUD TO CALL YOU HOME
AMERICA, AMERICA, THE PLACE I CALL MY OWN
I'M FROM A FOREIGN COUNTRY BUT HERE IS WHERE I'VE GROWN
AMERICA IS MY COUNTRY AND HERE MY ROOTS I'VE SOWN

TO THIS AMAZING COUNTRY, LAND OF
THE FREE AND THE BRAVE
I CAME WHEN I WAS LITTLE, A BETTER LIFE TO FIND
FROM POVERTY AND TYRANTS I FINALLY FEEL SAFE
GOD AND MY EFFORTS HELPED ME LEAVE MY OLD LIFE BEHIND

IT WELCOMES ALL THE PEOPLE WHO
FOR THEIR FREEDOM YEARN
AND MANY, MANY OTHERS WHO HAVE LITTLE TO EAT
AS SOON AS HERE WE SETTLE, WE HAVE A CHANCE TO LEARN
THAT WITH A MIGHTY EFFORT, LIFE HERE WILL BE A TREAT

AMERICA, AMERICA, I'M PROUD TO CALL YOU HOME
AMERICA, AMERICA, THE PLACE I CALL MY OWN
I'M FROM A FOREIGN COUNTRY BUT HERE IS WHERE I'VE GROWN
AMERICA IS THE COUNTRY WHERE MY ROOTS I HAVE SOWN

AS SOON AS WE ARE ABLE, ITS VASTNESS WE CAN SEE
ITS BEAUTY AND ITS BOUNTY FROM SEA TO SHINING SEA
SEEING ALL THESE BOUNDLESS TREASURES,
WE SOON ARE MADE AWARE
THAT WE CAN CALL THEM OURS, FOR ALL OF THEM WE SHARE

AMERICAN, THEY CALL ME AND I FEEL VERY PROUD
BEING A SON OF THIS COUNTRY MAKES ME STAND VERY TALL
THANKFUL FOR ALL ITS BOUNTY, I FEEL THE NEED TO SHOUT
"LONG LIVE THE GREATEST COUNTRY AND MAY IT NEVER FALL!"

AMERICA, AMERICA, I'M PROUD TO CALL YOU HOME
AMERICA, AMERICA, THE PLACE I CALL MY OWN
I'M FROM A FOREIGN COUNTRY BUT HERE IS WHERE I'VE GROWN
AMERICA IS MY COUNTRY AND HERE MY ROOTS I'VE SOWN

I'VE LOST MY MUSE

Where am I going
What am I doing
I wish I knew it
I want some answers

At times I'm certain
I will get there
If I'm persistent
and keep on working

I'm really trying
I have direction
But I'm not sure
if I'll get there

I keep on writing
I keep on thinking
I keep on stopping
I keep on blanking

She was my drive
my inspiration
That's why my mind
seems to go blank

I'm also sad
and quite discouraged
I'm sometimes mad
with our sad lives

I could keep going
and have direction
But all her problems
can't be my focus

We don't need sadness
in all my writings
It would be boring
to all my readers

But I'll keep at it
if time permits it
If my time gets here
my route will end

I need more drive
and much more focus
Where can I find that
without persistence

I need to give them
happy inspiration
They need some laughter
and happy thoughts

MY WORLD IS SHRINKING

My world is disappearing
I think it's quickly shrinking
That is what I am fearing
It is what I am thinking

I go to many places
Faces I look at thrice
But none of all those faces
I seem to recognize

Seeing friends gave me pleasure
Whenever I went out
But now there is no treasure
In being one of the crowd

It's Nature just fulfilling
A job that's not too kind
My friends it keeps on killing
Leaving me right behind

I know I should be happy
For leaving me alone
But I feel most unhappy
For not yet having gone

I know family surrounds me
But it is not enough
My friends I cannot see
And that is mighty tough

My children come around
To see me once in a while
But lately I have found
That with that I can't reconcile

I want to see them often
To chatter with them miles
But their schedules they can't soften
And that leaves me with no smiles

But I can understand
And I am pretty certain
That old age goes hand in hand
With becoming a burden

But Nature let's not blame
For my present situation
Because Nature is just the flame
Of our Lord's divine action

Only He has the choice
Of taking those He takes
He's the One with the voice
And He never makes mistakes

I'll forget my impatience
And wait for Him to call
I'll wait with equal patience
Seeing many of my friends fall

Real soon my time will come
And I will my friends see
That day I'll surely welcome
Chatting we soon will be

MY LIFE AS I'VE SEEN IT

Life has been good to me,
　　although I've had some years
　　　　when I wished I had not been born.

In my very early childhood,
　　I lost someone very close
　　　　who was our family tower.

But life continued on, as usual.
　　Some times were blissful
　　　　and other times were the worst.

Peers can be mean, at times,
　　And some of mine made
　　　　my life a living hell.

But life continued on, as usual.
　　Sometimes it was bearable
　　　　and other time unbearable.

School time was quite enjoyable
　　and I always made the best of it.
　　　　But it ended at an early age.

Because our family tower was gone,
　　my school fun ended for a while.
　　　　Boy, being poor can be a curse!

At ten, children are found
　　at school learning the three R's
　　　　and having fun with classmates.

But that pleasure is for the well-to-do
who have enough or more than enough
to live a nutritional existence.

The poor have to leave their schooling
to go out to find a job
to help support their family.

My childhood working years were few,
for I had to leave my village to become
an illegal alien in the United States of America.

Although the plan was to continue working
as soon as I reached my destination,
fate had other plans for me.

Because I was too young to work,
thanks to this land's child labor laws,
I had to continue my education.

Again, children can be quite mean,
even in this new environment,
for I had some bad experiences.

But life continued on, as usual.
Most of the time I had fun
but a few times were discouraging.

Adolescence can be worrisome
because, if fate is not on your side,
you can get in lots of trouble.

But fate was quite good to me,
as I sailed through my adolescence
without any of the usual problems

In my successful late teens,
someone became quite envious
and caused me trouble with the B. P.

Back to work I went, in Mexicali,
　　because some envious acquaintance
　　　　and the Border Patrol sent me back to Mexico.

My graduation was delayed for a year
　　and I lost track of my long-time classmates.
　　　　But I returned to graduate one year later.

College seemed to be unreachable
　　but, thanks to Mom and part-time jobs,
　　　　my tenacity pulled me through to graduation.

Marriage to the prettiest girl in the world
　　brought me joy and resolve to continue studying
　　　　and I finally earned my B. A. and M. A. Degrees.

Three beautiful daughters heightened my happiness,
　　as I saw them grow, graduate, earn their degrees
　　　　and marry three great sons-in-law.

They gave me seven beautiful grandchildren
　　whom we took care of, at times,
　　　　until disabilities and old age put a stop to it.

But life continues on, as usual,
　　with incurable disease, plenty of disabilities,
　　　　and dark clouds in the horizon.

While being a caregiver to my other half,
　　I wrote some stories that I've published
　　　　and some songs that I've recorded.

In between those stories and songs,
　　I wrote several poems
　　　　and my personal autobiography.

Hopefully, I plan to have all these published
　　before I become completely disabled,
　　　　as my wife has been for years.

And time continues moving forward, as usual,
without thinking or worrying one bit
about what it brings to all of us.

We have become sedimentary, more or less.
My wife and I cannot go anywhere together.
And I'll soon have more trouble walking.

Time keeps ambling on its way, as usual,
leaving some of us way behind,
crippled in limbs, minds and hearts.

We're just waiting for never-ending life
to leave us farther behind
and completely out of sight.

We'll say good-bye, forevermore,
to this beautiful life, cruel at times.
But, boy, how beautiful it is at times!

EMPTY AND DISGUSTED

EMPTY MY MIND HAS BEEN
EMPTY FOR QUITE A WHILE
DEVOID OF ANY IDEAS
ANY IDEAS TO WRITE ABOUT

EVER SINCE MY LAST MANUSCRIPT
I HAVE HAD NO NEW INSPIRATION
I TRY AND I TRY VERY OFTEN
TO GET SOMETHING ON PAPER

NOTHING ENTERS MY MIND
NOTHING WORTHWHILE TO WRITE ABOUT
COULD MY BRAIN HAVE RUN DRY?
HAVE ALL MY CELLS GONE BYE-BYE?

THAT CAN MEAN ONLY ONE THING
MY BATTERY HAS GONE DRY
IT COULD MEAN SOMETHING ELSE
MY DESIRE TO WRITE HAS WANED

I JUST WISH TO FORGET
THAT ALL I HAVE WRITTEN BEFORE
HAS BEEN A WASTE OF TIME
AND I DON'T HAVE IT IN ME

MAYBE I NEVER HAD IT BEFORE
AND I JUST CAME TO REALIZE IT
I DO FEEL THE NEED TO ENGAGE
IN SOMETHING TO KEEP ME BUSY

IF I DON'T HAVE SOMETHING TO DO
SOMETHING TO KEEP ME OCCUPIED
BOREDOM REALLY SETS IN
AND I FEEL COMPLETELY USELESS

WATCHING TV IS NOT AN OPTION
THERE'S NOTHING WORTHWHILE TO WATCH
IF IT'S NOT BASKETBALL OR THE NEWS
EVERYTHING SEEMS MONOTONOUS

BASKETBALL GAMES ARE FAR APART
AND THE NEWS ARE DISAPPOINTING
IF MY LAKERS DON'T WIN I'M DISGUSTED
AND MUELLER'S INVESTIGATION DRAGS ON

I WANT TRUMP TO BE FOUND GUILTY SOON
BECAUSE I AM CERTAIN HE IS
THE SOONER HE'S IMPEACHED OR RESIGNS
THE BETTER I AND MANY WILL FEEL

THE LONGER HE STAYS IN OFFICE
THE HIGHER THE RISK OF US GOING TO WAR
IF THAT HAPPENS OUR TROUBLES
WILL DISAPPEAR LIKE MAGIC

WE WILL BE GONE AND SO WILL THEY
WHOEVER IS LEFT ALIVE
WILL CONTINUE HAVING MORE PROBLEMS
I DON'T WANT TO BE ONE OF THEM

I'D RATHER BE ONE OF THE CASUALTIES
AND EVEN IF WE DON'T GO TO WAR
HE'LL MAKE OUR LIVES MORE MISERABLE
HE'S DONE SO MANY BAD THINGS

HE'LL BECOME ANOTHER PUTIN
THAT IS EXACTLY WHAT HE WANTS
TO RULE LIKE A DICTATOR
AND WE JUST CANNOT PERMIT IT

I HOPE MUELLER AND TRUMP'S REPUBLICANS
SEE THE REAL FUTURE UNDER HIM
THEY MUST FIND HIM GUILTY AND CHARGED
THEN HE'LL RESIGN OR BE IMPEACHED

OUR PROBLEMS WILL NOT DISAPPEAR
AS DEMOCRATS WILL STILL BE DOWN
THE REPUBLICANS HAVE ALWAYS BEEN
THE PARTY TO MAKE THE WEALTHY RICHER

THEY NEVER CARED FOR THE DOWNTRODDEN
THE POOR, THE PEOPLE OF COLOR
THOUGH THEY CLAIMED TO HAVE THE BEST MORALS
COMPARED TO OUR DEMOCRATIC FRIENDS

BUT NOW THOSE MORALS HAVE GONE
AND THEY WILL SUFFER FOR LOSING THEM
THEY WILL LOSE THE NEXT ELECTIONS
AND WE'LL GAIN CONTROL OF CONGRESS

OF COURSE, IT IS WISHFUL THINGKING
ON MANY OF MY DEMOCRAT ALLIES
BUT IT SURE LOOKS LIKE IT'LL HAPPEN
AND IF IT DOES, WHAT THEN?

HOW WILL OUR LIVES IMPROVE?
THAT THEY WILL, I AM CERTAIN
THEY SHOULD BE MUCH, MUCH BETTER
FOR EVERYONE EXCEPT FOR ME

COME THE NEXT ELECTION AND
I'LL PROBABLY BE GONE FOR GOOD
AT LEAST I WON'T BE COMPLAINING
ABOUT THE THINGS MR. TRUMP IS DOING

HE'LL GO ONE ROUTE AND I'LL GO ANOTHER
MY RELATIVES WILL SAVOR THAT
FOR THEY WON'T HAVE A DICTATORSHIP
WHICH WILL MAKE THEIR LIVES MORE NORMAL

HOPEFULLY, IT WILL BE MORE ENJOYABLE
I WILL OBSERVE THEM FROM ABOVE
AND BE CHEERING ON OUR VICTORY
FOR TRUMP WILL HAVE BEEN TRUMPED

THE REPUBLICANS WILL BE
LIKE SHEEP IN THE DEMOCRAT'S CORRAL
A FATE THEY WILL CERTAINLY DESERVE
FOR BACKING UP MR. TRUMP

AN INCOMPETENT, TWEETING HAWK
WHO DREAMED OF BEING ANOTHER PUTIN
OR PERHAPS EVEN A NEW ADOLPH HITLER
DOWN WITH PUTIN, HITLER AND TRUMP

THERE WILL BE SOME WHO'LL GET ANGRY
AS SOON AS THEY READ MY CRITIQUE
BUT I WARN THEM AND WANT THEM TO KNOW
THAT I'M SIMPLY EXPRESSING MY OPINION

I WANT THEM TO SIMPLY CONTROL THEIR ANGER
OR DISPLEASURE AT A DEMOCRAT'S FEELINGS
FOR, IF THE SHOE WERE ON THE OTHER FOOT,
THEY WOULD BE EXPRESSING THEIR OWN

THEY SHOULD TAKE IT WITH A GRAIN OF SALT
AND NOT LEARN MR. TRMP'S BAD HABIT OF
GETTING EVEN WHEN SOMEONE CRITICIZES HIM
BY VENTING HIS ANGER OVER SOME TWEETS

WHEN DEMOCRATS ARE IN POWER, I'LL SURELY HEAR
A LOT OF THE OTHER SIDE'S COMPLAINTS
THAT HAS BEEN THE USUAL NORM
THAT POLITICS HAS BEEN FOR YEARS

ALTHOUGH I MUST REMIND THEM
THAT NEVER HAVE WE HAD A MAN LIKE TRUMP
WHO DESIRES THE POWERS DICTATORS HAVE WIELDED
SO THAT HE CAN DO AS HE PLEASES

RIGHT NOW HIS GET-EVEN ASSAULTS
ARE MINOR AND INCONSEQUENTIAL
MANY CONSIDER HIM JUST A TWEETERING NERD
AND THEY PAY NO MIND TO HIS RAGES

BUT WE MUST NOT LET HIM SUCCEED
IN ACQUIRING THE POWER HE WANTS
BECAUSE THEN THOSE HARMLESS TWEETS
CAN BECOME LETHAL IN HIS ANGRY MOUTH

HE'LL PUT MANY PEOPLE IN DANGER
OR MANY WILL EVEN LOSE THEIR LIVES
JUST LIKE HIS VARIOUS HEROES ARE DOING
AMONG THEM, PUTIN, DUTARTE AND KIM JONG-UN

SO, DEMOCRATS AND REPUBLICAN COLLEAGUES,
LOOK OUT FOR THE FUTURE OF OUR COUNTRY
DON'T LET YOUR POLITICS ALLOW HIM
THE POWER HE SO DESPERATELY WISHES

IT'S BETTER TO BE SAVE THAN TO BE SORRY
WE CAN'T THINK THAT HE'S HARMLESS
HE'LL GET HIS POWER IF WE LET HIM
INSTEAD, LET'S RUSH HIS REAR OUT OF OFFICE

ABRUMADO DE DOLORES

Me levanto con dolores.
Mi cuerpo está ya en su ocaso.
Pienso en tantos horrores!
Quizás sea mi último paso.

Abrumado de dolores,
ya me siento abandonado.
Estoy lleno de rencores,
y estoy muy desesperado.

Esta vida que ahora llevo,
ya no la puedo aguantar.
Nada a la vida le debo,
y aún así, me quiere matar.

Ya me duele dondequiera,
y me molesta lo que siento.
Si así sigo, ¿qué me espera?
Ya quisiera estar muerto.

Tengo que aguantar la vida,
con toditos mis dolores.
Pa' cuidar a mi querida,
el amor de mis amores.

Aunque yo morirme quiera,
tengo que seguir viviendo.
Porque si yo me muriera,
se quedaría élla sufriendo.

Ayúdame en mi trance.
Sáname y dame quietud.
Haz que tu piedad me alcance,
con gracia y buena salud.

Es lo único que pido,
Señor misericordioso.
Ya me siento muy perdido.
Por favor, sé más piadoso.

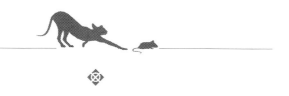

AHORA A USTEDES LES TOCA

Ahora que estamos ancianos, estamos como bebitos.
No podemos hacer nada de lo que antes hacíamos.
Recordamos que hace años ésto les pasaba a ustedes.
Sus piernitas les fallaban, comer solas no podían.
Pero no se preocupaban pues tenían mucha ayuda.
Las cargábamos en brazos para ir de un lado a otro.
Cuando tenían mucha hambre, les servíamos su comida.
Y con una cucharita, en la boca se la dábamos.
Ya cuando más grandecitas, menos nos necesitaban.
La comida les servíamos y solas se la comían.
Cuando sus necesidades se les antojaba hacerlas,
Estábamos siempre listos para lavar sus pañales.
Cuando aún mas grandecitas, al baño las llevábamos.
Y ahí ustedes solitas, sus necesidades hacían.
De bebitas se enfermaban y al médico las llevábamos.
Si no, medicinas caseras, con amor les aplicábamos.
Los papeles se han cambiado y ahora somos los bebitos.
Ahora Dios nos ha quitado dones de la gente joven.
Por eso necesitamos que nos presten su asistencia.
No podemos caminar ni podemos pensar claro.
Las piernas ya no obedecen las órdenes del cerebro.
Los mensajes de la mente muy a menudo se pierden.
Los ojos, pies y manos no los saben decifrar.
Nuestro hablar es menos claro y estamos poco sordos.
Ahora a ustedes les toca llevarnos de un lado a otro.
Les toca hablarnos mas fuerte y escucharnos con cuidado.
Pronto no vamos a estar para ya no molestarlas

No tendrán que preocuparse ni tendrán que estar al tanto,
De llevarnos para allá ni traernos para acá.
Ni tendrán que gritarnos para oir lo que nos dicen.
Ni poner mucha atención para oir lo que digamos.
Pero no nos abandonen mientras estemos viviendo,
Aunque no seamos muy "vivos" y casi todo nos falle.
Sabemos que sus quehaceres o quizás sea la distancia,
O quizás ya sus familias, visitarnos no permitan.
No creemos que el desamor ni la falta de interés,
Las mantenga tan lejanas y además despreocupadas.
No sabemos que será pero a Dios se lo dejamos.

SOLO ME SIENTO

HACE TIEMPO QUE SOLO ME SIENTO
AUNQUE HA ESTADO MI AMOR A MI LADO
HA PERDIDO EL DON DEL PENSAMIENTO
Y TAMBIÉN EL DE HABLAR HA DEJADO

A NINGÙN LADO VA ÉLLA CONMIGO
PORQUE HA PERDIDO EL MOVIMIENTO
SU APOYO EN TODO YA HE PERDIDO
PORQUE YA NO USA EL PENSAMIENTO

LAS COSAS QUE JUNTO HACÍAMOS
EN LA MENTE LAS LLEVO PRESENTES
LA VIDA GOZANDO REÍAMOS
EN REUNIÓN CON MUCHÍSIMA GENTE

AHORA SOLO CON MI AMOR LA PASO
A VECES CON POCOS FAMILIARES
ALEGRES LOS RATOS SON ESCASOS
SIN VISITAS A OTROS LUGARES

A MENUDO A LAS TIENDAS PUEDO IRME
PERO SOLA NO LA DEJO EN CASA
APENADO NO DEBO SENTIRME
PUES CON SU NANA NADA LE PASA

AL VOLVER, SUELO VERLA SENTADA
SUS OJOS EN LOS MÍOS REPOSAN
AL VERME SE MIRA ENCANTADA
SUS OJOS DE ALEGRÍA CREO QUE GOZAN

LAS DICHAS DE LOS TIEMPOS DE ANTAÑO
SIGUEN MUY CLARAS EN MI MEMORIA
SI LAS DISFRUTARA EN ESTOS AÑOS
AÚN ME SENTIRÍA EN PLENA GLORIA

MAS NO HAY QUE DEMASIADO QUEJARME
PUES JUNTOS ESTAMOS TODAVÍA
ÉLLA NO HA DEJADO DE AMARME
ME ALEGRA SABER QUE ES TODA MÍA

LA SOLEDAD QUE AHORA SIENTO
SE AMINORA AL VERLA AÚN VIVITA
OLVIDO MIS PENAS AL MOMENTO
Y ME ALEGRO, AL MENOS POR AHORITA

POR UN TIEMPO ASÍ SEGUIREMOS
GOZANDO LA POCA ALEGRÍA
QUE YO CREO QUE AÚN MERECEMOS
HASTA QUE LLEGUE EL FUNESTO DÍA

MIENTRAS TANTO, VIVIRÉ LA VIDA
LO MEJOR QUE DIOS ME LO PERMITA
AL LADO DE MI MUJER QUERIDA
MIENTRAS EL SEÑOR NO ME LA QUITA

MI MUNDO SE ESTÁ ENCOGIENDO

MI MUNDO SE ESTÁ ENCOGIENDO
CREO QUE SE ESTÁ ACABANDO
ESO LO HE ESTADO VIENDO
ES LO QUE HE ESTADO PENSANDO

AL SALIR VEO A LA GENTE
A VER SI A ALGUIEN CONOZCO
PERO EN MI ANCIANA MENTE
YA A NADIE RECONOZCO

A AMIGOS PODÍA VER
EN TODOS MIS RECORRIDOS
PERO TENGO QUE COMPRENDER
QUE ÉLLOS YA SE HAN IDO

SERÁ LA NATURALEZA
QUIEN SU CHAMBA ESTÁ HACIENDO
CAUSANDO ASÍ LA TRISTEZA
QUE AHORITA ESTOY SINTIENDO

DEBO DE ESTAR CONTENTO
PORQUE NO ME HA LLEVADO
PERO ESTOY DESCONTENTO
PORQUE A MÍ ME HA OLVIDADO

MIS AMIGOS SE HAN IDO
Y TRISTEZA SE SIENTE
TENGO A MIS MÁS QUERIDOS
MAS ME SIENTO CARECIENTE

MIS GENTES VIENEN A VERME
PERO EN MUY CORTO RATITO
HE LLEGADO A CONVENCERME
DE QUE ESO ES MUY POQUITO

QUISIERA QUE SÍ PUDIERAN
MUCHITO MÁS TIEMPO VERME
PUES BIEN SÉ QUE SI QUISIERAN
PODRÍAN BIEN COMPLACERME

PERO TODO LO COMPRENDO
PORQUE ESTOY MUY SEGURO
DE QUE ANCIANOS VIENEN SIENDO
UN CARGO BASTANTE DURO

NO HAY QUE LA CULPA ECHARLE
NUNCA A LA NATURALEZA
CULPA A DIOS VOY A DARLE
POR SU DIVINA GRANDEZA

SÓLO ÉL TIENE LA OPCIÓN
DE LLEVARSE A QUIEN LE TOCA
SÓLO DE ÉL ES LA DECISIÓN
Y ÉL NUNCA SE EQUIVOCA

MI IMPACIENCIA OLVIDARÉ
Y CON CALMA ESPERARÉ
EL ESCOGIDO PRONTO SERE
Y CON DIOS PRONTO ME IRÉ

MUY PRONTITO ME TOCARÁ
IR A VER A MIS AMIGOS
CADA UNO SE ARRIMARÁ
A HACER CHARLA CONMIIGO

ESPERAR, ESPERAR, ESPERAR

ESPERAR AHORA Y SIEMPRE ES UNA AGONÍA.
DESDE ANTES DE NACER HASTA EL DÍA DE MORIR,
TIENE QUE HABER PACIENCIA, ALGO QUE NO TENÍA.
PERO AHORA QUE ESTOY VIEJO LA EMPIEZO A SENTIR.

DESDE QUE ESTABA ADENTRO DE MI QUERIDA MADRE,
YO QUERÍA YA SALIRME A CONOCER EL MUNDO.
ANSIABA CON EL ALMA CONOCER A MI PADRE.
SALIR A LA AVENTURA, LO SENTÍA MUY PROFUNDO.

DESPUÉS DE HABER NACIDO, ME COMÍA LA IMPACIENCIA.
HABLAR CON TODO EL MUNDOI, ERA MI GRAN DESEO.
CORRER POR DONDEQUIERA, QUERÍA CON INSISTENCIA.
PERO ES QUE NO PODÍA, AHORA SÍ LO VEO.

CORRER HACIA LA ESCUELA, A MI HERMANA VEÍA.
ANTES DE IRSE, MI HERMANA PEQUEÑA LLORABA.
—HA DE SER MUY HERMOSA LA ESCUELA—YO CREÍA.
—¡YO TAMBIÉN QUIERO IR!—A MENUDO GRITABA.

DESPUÉS GANAS TENÍA DE DEJAR LA PRIMARIA.
LA ESCUELA ME GUSTABA PERO QUERÍA AVANZAR.
OÍA LO QUE PASABA ALLÁ EN LA SECUNDARIA,
Y MÁS GANAS ME DABAN DE IR A AVERIGUAR.

TODITO LO QUE OÍA SALIÓ SER LA VERDAD.
¡CÓMO ME DIVERTÍ EN LA PREPARATORIA!
HORAS Y DÍAS FELICES LAS TUVE EN CANTIDAD.
ESTANDO EN LA ESCUELA, VIVÍA EN LA GLORIA.

POR ESO YA DESEABA IRME A LA UNIVERSIDAD.
OÍA TANTAS COSAS QUE YA QUERÍA LLEGAR.
DESEABA ILUSTRARME, ILUSTRARME DE VERDAD.
DE LA PREPARATORIA, YA ME QUERÍA GRADUAR.

LOGRÉ YO REGISTRARME EN LA UNIVERSIDAD.
Y ESPERÉ MI DIPLOMA RÁPIDO RECIBIR.
LE ENTRÉ A MIS ESTUDIOS CON GRAN INTENSIDAD,
Y DE UN DÍA PARA OTRO, LA PUDE CONSEGUIR.

YA TENIENDO TRABAJO, LINDA CHAVA ENCONTRÉ.
YA QUERÍA CASARME. NO QUERÍA ESPERAR.
MAS EN POQUITO TIEMPO NOS PUDIMOS CASAR.
LUEGO, TRES LINDAS HIJAS JUNTOS PUDIMOS CRIAR.

SABÍA QUE EN POCO TIEMPO SE IBAN A ENAMORAR.
CASARSE EN VARIOS AÑOS NO QUISIERON ESPERAR,
Y, SIN PERDER MÁS TIEMPO, SE FUERON A CASAR.
Y AQUÍ, A LOS DOS SOLITOS, NOS QUISIERON DEJAR.

VINIERON NIETECITOS NUESTRA VIDA A ENDULZAR.
LA CHAMBA DE NIÑEROS NO SE PUDO ESPERAR.
POR AÑOS, A LOS NIETOS LOS PUDIMOS GOZAR.
MAS SABÍAMOS QUE EL GOZO NO NOS IBA A DURAR.

EL CRECER DE LOS NIÑOS NO PUDO ESPERAR.
AL CRECER LOS MORRITOS, LA CHAMBA SE ACABÓ.
LA EDAD Y MALES NUESTROS VINIERON A APAGAR,
LA LUZ DE AQUEL GOZO QUE PRONTO TERMINÓ.

ESTOS ÚLTIMOS AÑOS, LLENO DE ANSIEDAD,
HE ESTADO MIS PROBLEMAS QUERIENDO SUPERAR.
HAN SIDO DEPRIMENTES, TAN DUROS DE VERDAD,
QUE SOLUCIÓN A ÉLLOS TENGO QUE ESPERAR.

QUE ALIVIE A MI AMORCITO DE SU ENFERMEDAD,
A MI DIOSITO SANTO YO LE VOY A ROGAR.
MAS SÉ QUE ESPERAREMOS POR UNA ETERNIDAD,
PUES DE ESA ENFERMEDAD NUNCA SE VA A ALIVIAR.

POR HOY, MUY IMPACIENTE TENDRÉ QUE ESPERAR,
QUE DIOS A MI AMORCITO LA QUIERA ALIVIAR.
QUE ESE MILAGRO ME HAGA, YO LE VOY A PEDIR.
QUIZÁS EN POCO TIEMPO ME LO PUEDA CUMPLIR.

HAZAÑA INHUMANA

MUCHOS NIÑOS SE ENCUENTRAN DESAMPARADOS
SÓLO POR CAPRICHO DE UN PRESIDENTE
DE SUS PADRES SE ENCUENTRAN SEPARADOS
POR UN HOMBRE INHUMANO E INCONSCIENTE

ENCERRADOS COMO VILES PRISIONEROS
POR TODITO EL PAÍS DESPARRAMADOS
NO LOS QUIERE SÓLO PORQUE NO SON GÜEROS
QUIERE QUE DE EL PAÍS SEAN DEPORTADOS

ESOS NIÑOS MUY MAL TIEMPO ESTÁN PASANDO
LLORANDO POR SUS PADRES CONSTANTEMENTE
TODO ESTO LOS HA DE ESTAR TRAUMATIZANDO
TANTO QUE LES PUEDE AFECTAR LA MENTE

NO PUEDEN VER A TANTOS NIÑOS SUFRIENDO
POR ESO MUCHA GENTE ANDA PROTESTANDO
REUNIÓN DE FAMILIAS ESTÁN PIDIENDO
NO QUIEREN VER A NIÑOS SOLOS RODANDO

CONGRESISTAS TIENEN LOS OJOS CERRADOS
CERRADOS A LO QUE TRUMP ESTÁ HACIENDO
SI USARAN EL PODER QUE LES HAN DADO
YA ESTUVIERA EL SEÑOR TRUMP ENCARCELADO

YA EN LA CÁRCEL SERÁ PRONTO REEMPLAZADO
POR ALGUIEN QUE QUIZÁS SEA MÁS CONSCIENTE
QUE A LA CONSTITUCIÓN SEA MÁS APEGADO
QUE DE NUESTRO BIENESTAR ESTÉ PENDIENTE

MAS NO CREO QUE EL SEÑOR PENCE SE COMPARE
CON NINGUNO DE LOS PREVIOS PRESIDENTES
NO CREO QUE DESTROZOS AL PAÍS REPARE
TEMO QUE SEA IGUAL DE INCONSCIENTE

TENDRÁ QUE ENMENDAR TANTOS DESHECHOS
QUE EL SEÑOR TRUMP HIZO CON NUESTROS ALIADOS
LO TORCIDO TENDRÁ QUE PONER DERECHOS
PORQUE NO ES UNO SINO DEMASIADOS

TRATADOS CON ALIADOS, YA DESTROZADOS
Y LOS BERRINCHES QUE CON FAMILIAS CAUSÓ
SON MALES QUE FUERON POR ÉL APROBADOS
QUIZÁS NO LE GUSTARON PERO ÉL CALLÓ

ESPERO YO ESTAR MUY EQUIVOCADO
Y QUE PENCE APRENDA DE LO SUCEDIDO
QUE NO SEA IGUAL A TRUMP DE MALVADO
Y QUE RECUPERE LO QUE HEMOS PERDIDO

EL PRESTIGIO COMO EJEMPLAR DEMOCRACIA
DE ALGÚN MODO PODREMOS RECUPERAR
LA PERDIMOS EN EUROPA Y EN EL ASIA
TEMO QUE NOS DEJARON DE RESPETAR

SOMOS LA NACIÓN MÁS RICA Y PODEROSA
PERO SIN PRESTIGIO ESO NO VA A DURAR
SI ENTRAMOS EN UNA ACCIÓN BELICOSA
NUESTROS ALIADOS NOS VAN A ABANDONAR

SI LA ENEMISTAD ENTRE PAÍSES REVIVE
Y UNA NUEVA GUERRA LLEGA A ESTALLAR
SI ALGUNA GENTE EN EL MUNDO SOBREVIVE
ENTRE ESOS, NOSOTROS NO VAMOS A ESTAR

MI DIOSITO, TU AYUDA NECESITAMOS
DALES CORAZÓN A LOS REPUBLICANOS
QUE EL PROBLEMA DE LOS NIÑOS RESOLVAMOS
Y QUE DEL SEÑOR TRUMP YA NOS DESPIDAMOS

QUIZÁS TENGAMOS GUERRA

LA VIDA SE NOS VA
SE ACERCA YA EL OCASO
LA VIDA SÓLO DA
EN EL PESCUEZO UN LAZO

EL PRECIO QUE AHORA TIENE
ME HA TUMBADO ILUSIONES
ME ASUSTA LO QUE VIENE
TRISTES PERTURBACIONES

NADA PUEDO COMPRAR
MI PENSIÓN DA MUY POCO
DONDE IRÉ APARAR
VOY AVOLVERME LOCO

YA NO HAY NADA BARATO
LOS PRECIOS VAN SUBIENDO
ME HAN COLMADO EL PLATO
ME ESTÁN ENLOQUECIENDO

POR FAVOR, MI DIOSITO
CUÍDAME DE LA RUINA
YA ME DUELE POQUITO
NO CLAVES MÁS LA ESPINA

SUBIÓ MUCHO LA RENTA
TAMBIÉN LA ASEGURANZA
LA VIDA ES MUY HAMBRIENTA
PA' NADA NOS ALCANZA

YO SÉ QUE ESTAMOS VIEJOS
PRONTO HEMOS DE MORIR
YA ESTAMOS LOS AÑEJOS
CANSADOS DE VIVIR

QUIZÁS TENGAMOS GUERRA
SE ACERCA LA OCASIÓN
PARA ESTA VIDA PERRA
SERA LA SOLUCIÓN

SÉ LO QUE VA A PASAR
ESTOY CASI SEGURO
VAMOS A DESTROZAR
DE TODOS EL FUTURO

LOS NIÑOS NO SABRÁN
(POR CULPA DEL DEMONIO)
TAMPOCO GOZARÁN
LO QUE ES EL MATRIMONIO

SE IRÁN SIN CONOCER
Y SIN HABER PROBADO
EL AMOR DE MUJER
NI LO QUE ES SER AMADO

TODO ESO LO SENTÍ
LO GOCÉ A LO PROFUNDO
PERO, AY, POBRE DE MÍ
SE ACABARÁ MI MUNDO

OJALÁ EL PRESIDENTE
CAMBIE DE PARECER
Y QUE TENGA PRESENTE
LO QUE VA A SUCEDER

NADIE EN SU SANA MENTE
QUISIERA YA MORIR
QUEREMOS, FRANCAMENTE,
QUEDARNOS A VIVIR

PERO UNO NACE UN DÍA
SIN SABER SU DESTINO
ES EL SEÑOR QUIEN GUÍA
SU OBSCURO CAMINO

SERES SIEMPRE SEREMOS
POR ALGUIEN CONTROLADOS
Y TODOS NOS MOVEMOS
POR DIFERENTES LADOS

CUANDO EL SEÑOR DECIDE
QUE EL DÍA SE TE HA LLEGADO
EL SOLAMENTE PIDE
Y YA ESTÁS A SU LADO

SI ESA GUERRA ESTALLA
Y ME TOCA LA MUERTE
QUE CON DIOS YO ME VAYA
SERÁ MI BUENA SUERTE

NO HABRÁ QUE PREOCUPARME
EN COSAS DE LA VIDA
NO TENDRÉ QUE COMPRARME
ESA CARA COMIDA

QUE EL DINERO NO ALCANZA
QUE YA NO HAY QUE CENAR
SIEMPRE CON LA ESPERANZA
DE LOTERÍAS GANAR

EL PROBLEMA ES INMENSO
DA GRAN PERTURBACIÓN
ESO ES BANSTANTE TENSO
ES DAÑO AL CORAZÓN

POR ESO, QUE YA MANDE
LA GUERRA A MATARME
PARA QUE EL ME MANTENGA
Y YA NO PREOCUPARME

DESPUES YO VIVIRE
GOZANDO DE SU GLORIA
LA GUERRA—PENSARE
QUE FUE MI GRAN VICTORIA

PERO YO ESTOY SEGURO
QUE VAN MUCHO A SUFRIR
LOS QUE PARA UN FUTURO
PUEDAN SOBREVIVIR

ABE AND BENITO

OF ALL THE REAL AMERICANS, NO ONE HAS GAINED MORE FAME
THAN TWO OF OUR GREAT GIANTS, WHOSE
LIFE GOALS WERE THE SAME
ALTHOUGH ONE CROSSED THE RIO GRANDE,
THESE TWO MEN NEVER MET
FOR LADY LUCK HAD INTERFERED AND
THEIR FATE HAD BEEN SET

THEIR NATIONS TORN ASUNDER BY
THEIR OWN PEOPLE'S DISCORD
LINCOLN WAS WORRIED THAT THE SOUTH
WOULD BREAK AWAY FROM THE NORTH
WHILE THE CONQUEST OF MEXICO THE
FRENCH HAD BOLDLY PLANNED
FOR LOUIS NAPOLEON WAS SURE HE'D EASILY TAKE THE LAND

DON BENITO'S REQUEST FOR HELP WAS SENT TO HONEST ABE
WHO HAD TO, WITH REGRETS, REFUSE
'TIL THE COUNTRY WAS SAFE
BUT SOON AFTER THE REBEL TROOPS
HIS TROOPS BEGAN TO ROUT
HIS FULL ATTENTION, THEN, WAS TURNED
TO THE COUNTRY DOWN SOUTH

BENITO'S TROOPS WERE SOON TO SEE
THE HATED FRENCH DEPART
AS MAXINE AND CARLOTA SAW THEIR SHORT RULE FALL APART
A MAN NAMED BOOTHE CUT SHORT THE
LIFE OF OUR HONEST ABE
BEFORE HE'D SEE HIS COUNTRY SAFE
AND FREEDOM FOR THE SLAVE

BENITO WAS TO LOSE HIS LIFE A FEW YEARS AFTER ABE
BUT HE LIVED LONG ENOUGH TO SEE
THAT HIS COUNTRY WAS SAFE
THOUGH BLESSED WITH GREAT MEN THE
U. S. AND MEXICO HAVE BEEN,
MEN LIKE JUÁREZ AND LINCOLN WILL NEVER AGAIN BE SEEN

AMERICA AND MEXICO WOULD DEEPLY GRIEVE THEIR LOSS
THEY KNEW THEY HAD LOST TWO GREAT
MEN WHO DIED FOR THEIR CAUSE
HAD THESE TWO GREAT MEN MET, IT IS
WITH CERTAINTY ASSUMED
THAT A CLOSE FRIENDSHIP, WITHOUT DOUBT,
IN NO TIME WOULD HAVE BLOOMED

¿DE DÓNDE VINE Y A DÓNDE VOY?

De dónde vine y a dónde voy
Preguntas que se las llevó el aire
De lo que muy seguro estoy
Es que naci de mi santa madre

Mis padres me vieron nacer
Y a menudo me han contado
El cómo y dónde pude saber
Así es que estoy bien enterado

Lo que yo quisiera saber
Es a dónde y con quién voy a ir
Eso me lo quisiera aprender
Antes de que me vaya a morir

Sabiendo a donde me voy a ir
Con tiempo estaré preparado
Así el dia que llegue a morir
No me iré muy asustado

Dicen que tengo que escoger
Ya sea el cielo o el infierno
Por ahora no lo tengo que hacer
Hay mucho tiempo aún estoy tierno

Si quiero la vida disfrutar
Sin pensar en los mandamientos
De seguro que voy a pecar
Con actos y con lod pensamientos

Por cuál camino voy a seguir
De eso ni yo estoy muy seguro
A Diosito voy a pedir
Que me convierta en hombre puro
Que no me deje mi alma perder

Pues verlo un día es mi anhelo
Quiero su absolución merecer
Para estar con Él en el cielo

Dame, Señor, mucha devoción
Para seguir tus mandamientos
Por mis pecados pido perdón
Con sincero arrepentimiento

DORMIR NO HE PODIDO

DORMIR BASTANTE NO HE PODIDO
CREO QUE YA TENGO VARIAS SEMANAS
DORMIR SÓLO OCHO HORAS YO PIDO
DE DORMIR MUY BIEN YA TENGO GANAS

NO SÉ QUÉ ME MANTIENE DESPIERTO
A VECES TRES O CUATRO HORAS DUERMO
YO SÉ BIEN, Y ESTOY EN LO CIERTO,
QUE SI NO DUERMO BIEN YO ME ENFERMO

SÉ QUE HE VIVIDO MUCHOS AÑOS
Y DORMIR MENOS HORAS SE ESPERA
MAS DORMIR COMO EN AÑOS DE ANTAÑO
ES LO QUE CON GANAS YO QUISIERA

PERO CREO QUE SÍ SÉ LO QUE TENGO
APARTE DE YA SER UN VIEJITO
PENSANDO EN COSAS ME MANTENGO
POR ESO ES QUE DUERMO TAN POQUITO

SE ME QUITA UN POCO EL INSOMNIO
TOMANDO MEDICINAS MALDITAS
QUE PUEDEN SER EL MISMO DEMONIO
PORQUE VUELVEN A LAS GENTES ADICTAS

PERO SI EL SUEÑO NO LO REPONGO
TENDRÉ ALGÚN EFECTO SECUNDARIO
MAL DE OTRAS ENFERMEDADES ME PONGO
Y EL INSOMNIO SE HARÁ MÁS A DIARIO

MI SISTEMA IMUNE ME HA FALLADO
PORQUE DÍAS SIN DORMIR HE DURADO
DOS VECES ANEMIA ME HA PEGADO
DÍAS EN EL HOSPITAL HE PASADO

YA POR VIEJO NO DUERMO MUY BIEN
PUES ME ABRUMAN BASTANTE MIS PENAS
COSAS SIN IMPORTANCIA TAMBIÉN
SE AGREGAN A TODOS MIS PROBLEMAS

UN POEMA ME VIENE A LA MENTE
Y DE ÉLLA NO LA PUEDO SACAR
MELODÍAS LLEGAN DE REPENTE
Y POR NADA LAS PUEDO DESCARDAR

ME LEVANTO A ESCRIBIRLAS LUEGUITO
PARA PODER LA CALMA ALCANSAR
LUEGO PUEDO DORMIR UN POQUITO
Y SÓLO ASÍ PUEDO DESCANSAR

SÓLO QUE ÉSTO ME PASA SEGUIDO
Y NO SÉ CUANDO VAYA A TERMINAR
MUCHAS VECES A DIOS YO LE PIDO
QUE MIS MALES YA ME QUIERA QUITAR

MUCHOS AÑOS YO YA HE VIVIDO
Y YA NO QUIERO VIVIR MUCHO MÁS
QUE ME LLEVE CON ÉL LE HE PEDIDO
PARA QUE POR FIN VIVA YO EN PAZ

QUE EL DÍA QUE ME LLEVE CONSIGO
QUE SE LLEVE TAMBIÉN A MI AMOR
PARA QUE SE VAYA ÉLLA CONMIGO
SE LO HE PEDIDO CON MUCHO FERVOR

AMOR DE MADRE

¿Has pensado alguna vez
por qué una niña juega con muñecas,
y aún pequeña, en casarse sueña?
¿Por qué de esposa en su nuevo hogar
Añora y espera dar a luz a un niño?

Es que Dios con su poder divino
Le ha enseñado que ese es su destino.
Élla sabe, en lo más profundo,
en la profundidad de su mente,
que su Dios la envió a este mundo
para eso exactamente.

Pasa el tiempo y, cierto día
¡Felicidades! —el médico augura.
¡Yo ya sabía lo que Dios me envía!
—dice élla con sutil dulzura.
—Desde hace días que estoy segura,
—agrega luego, llena de alegría.

Por fin llega el día dichoso.
Su corazón late al ver a su nene.
Siente que no hay día más glorioso.
Y, además, piensa que élla tiene
al bebé más lindo y más precioso.

Pasa el tienpo y más hijos llegan.
Con las mismas ansias los espera.
Crecen, se casan y consigo llevan
el amor de una madre verdadera

A MI MADRE

¡Si supieras lo que siento al mirarte!
¡Se me sale el corazón de tanto amor!
Y recuerdo que pa' siempre he de adorarte,
Evitándote cualquier mayor dolor.

La vida hace varios años tú me diste.
Me criaste y me mimaste con ternura.
Con cariño enderesarme bien supiste,
Pues mi vida conoce poca amargura

En palabras que me diste he pensado.
Frases sabias que escuché de noche y día:
—En lo que hagas y que digas ten cuidado
Que en el mundo en abundancia hay villanía

Ten cuidado que tus obras nunca ofendan
Ni a tu prójimo ni a Dios en las alturas
Que palabras de tu boca nunca enciendan
La fogata de un gran odio y de amarguras—

He tratado de seguir tus instrucciones,
Aunque a veces esta vida es traicionera.
A menudo me he topado con traiciones,
Que me han hecho reaccionar de mal manera.

A pesar de que la vida ha sido dura,
He tratado de llevar vida ejemplar.
Yo te digo con modestia humilde y pura,
Que gracias a Dios y a ti llegué a triunfar.

Gracias, Dios, por ese bello amor de madre,
Que ha servido para guiar mi caminar.
¿Que podría yo hacer ahora que soy padre,
Sin sus frases que hoy en día me pueden guiar?

Para siempre en este mundo seas bendita,
Al igual que en la presencia del Señor.
Te mereces esto y más, mi mamacita,
Porque al criarme tú me hiciste un gran favor.

Si algún día te sorprende a ti la muerte,
Y te arranca de nosotros el Creador,
Te prometo en mi tristeza ser muy fuerte,
Recordando tus palabras y tu amor.

Pensaré que al paraíso ya te fuiste,
Y que gozas de la vida allá en la Gloria.
Además, recordaré lo que me diste,
Y orgulloso adoraré yo tu memoria.

Preferible es gozar de tu existencia.
Pediré que Dios te dé una larga vida.
Que ilumine este hogar con tu presencia,
Porque eres para mí la más querida.

Me complace demostrarte mi cariño.
Esto y más tú te mereces con razón.
He tenido tu calor desde que niño,
Y por eso me robaste el corazón.

TENGO GANAS DE IRME

TENGO GANAS DE A ALGÚN LADO IRME
LAS GANAS ME DAN DE VEZ EN CUANDO
MÁS BIEN TENGO GANAS DEL HOGAR SALIRME
ME VIENEN CUANDO CANSADO ANDO

LOS PROBLEMAS ME HACEN SENTIR ESO
O SERÁN LOS MALES QUE ME SIGUEN
DE ESOS MALES SIENTO YA SU PESO
O SON LOS DIABLOS QUE ME PERSIGUEN

NO SÉ BIEN PERO ESTOY CONFUNDIDO
LO QUE SÍ SÉ ES QUE YA NO AGUANTO
HACE TIEMPO QUE ASÍ ME HE SENTIDO
ES QUE YA MI CRUZ ME PESA TANTO

EN VERDAD NO SÉ LO QUE VOY A HACER
AUNQUE SÉ QUE NO PUEDO HACER NADA
TENDRÉ QUE AGUANTAR ESTE PADECER
CON VALOR, CON CAPA Y CON ESPADA

MI DIOS SABRÁ QUE HACER CON MI CASO
SI MALES MEJOREN O SE EMPEOREN
SEGUIRÉ EL CAMINO PASO A PASO
AUNQUE ESTOS OJOS SIEMPRE LLOREN

SI A DIOS PIDO QUE TENGA COMPASIÓN
Y QUE PUEDA SEGUIR ADELANTE
LO PIDIRÉ DE TODO CORAZÓN
SI NO, QUE ÉL ME LLAME AL INSTANTE

YO BIEN SÉ QUE TENGO MUCHOS CARGOS
Y SÉ QUE TENGO QUE MANEJARLOS
AUNQUE SEAN DEMASIADOS ENCARGOS
NO PIENSO, POR NADA, OLVIDARLOS

A CADA PASITO ME ENCRUDEZCO
AL PENSAR QUE QUIERO ESCAPARME
DE TODOS LOS MALES QUE PADEZCO
PERO SÉ QUE NO PODRÉ SAFARME

LO QUE VOY A HACER ES AGUANTARME
Y HACERLE FRENTE A ESTA VIDA
PORQUE EL SEÑOR NO QUERRÁ LLEVARME
AUNQUE DE RODILLAS SE LO PIDA

SEÑOR, QUIERO QUE YA ME DEJES IR
O QUE MIS MALES DE MÍ AHUYENTES
PORQUE SÉ MUY BIEN QUE SÓLO AL MORIR
MIS PESARES ESTARÁN AUSENTES

PERDONA MIS MALOS PENSAMIENTOS
Y HAZME QUE LOS SAQUE DE MI MENTE
TEN EN CUENTA YA MIS SENTIMIENTOS
QUE A MIS MALES PUEDA HACERLES FRENTE

REFUERZA MI DÉBIL FORTALEZA
PARA MEJOR CUIDAR A MI AMADA
MEJOR VIDA DALE A MI TERESA
Y NUNCA TE PEDIRÉ YA NADA

¿QUÉ ES EL AMOR?

EL AMOR ES ALGO MUY BONITO
QUE SE ENCUENTRA EN NUESTROS CORAZONES
ES ALGO POR MI DIOS MUY BENDITO
QUE CONDUCE A MUY GRANDES ACCIONES

A UN ESPOSO EN BUENO LO CONVIERTE
POR AMOR ES UN PADRE EXCELENTE
POR LOS SUYOS BUEN PADRE SE SIENTE
CARIÑOSO, ALEGRE Y PACIENTE

NUNCA QUIERE DEJARLOS SOLITOS
PORQUE HACERLO LE CAUSA LA MUERTE
A MENUDO LES PLANTA BESITOS
DE ÉLLOS NUNCA DESEA ESTAR AUSENTE

SI SU HERMANO SE ENOJA Y LO OFENDE
LO PERDONA Y LE VUELVE LA CARA
CONTRA EL MUNDO SIEMPRE LO DEFIENDE
CON AMOR ÉL LO AYUDA Y LO AMPARA

DA AUXILIO, A ENFERMOS VISITA
DA LIMOSNA A LA IGLESIA, AL MENDIGO
A VECINOS A SU CASA INVITA
Y A JESÚS LLEVA ÉL SIEMPRE CONSIGO

HACE TODO CON UNA DULZURA
QUE CONMUEVE A MIL CORAZONES
ALEGRAR, REPARTIR SU TERNURA
SON SUS MÁS FERVIENTES INTENCIONES

SI TODITA LA GENTE SINTIERA
ESE AMOR TAN SINCERO Y PROFUNDO
QUÉ BONITO, QUÉ RECHULO FUERA
QUÉ DISTINTO SERÍA NUESTRO MUNDO

NO HABRÍA NI UNA CLASE DE MALDAD
VIVIRÍAMOS TODOS COMO HERMANOS
REINARÍA VERDADERA HERMANDAD
SENTIMIENTOS SERÍAN TODOS SANOS

QUE RECHULO SERÍA NUESTRO MUNDO
DONDE HABRÍA AMOR EN CANTIDAD
CON AMOR TAN SINCERO Y PROFUNDO
GOZARÍAMOS LA PAZ DE VERDAD

PERDONE USTED

PERDONE USTED MI GRAN ATREVIMIENTO
PERO ES QUE YA NO AGUANTO ESTA EMOCIÓN
ES QUE ALGO MUY LINDO POR USTED SIENTO
QUE ME HA ESTADO SANGRANDO EL CORAZÓN

HABLARLE DE MI AMOR ME HE ANIMADO
CON RIESGO DE EXPONERME A UN RECHAZÓN
PERO HACE TANTO QUE LA HE AMADO
QUE CREO QUE ENFERMO ESTOY DEL CORAZÓN

YO SÉ QUE NO TENGO NINGÚN DERECHO
DE ABRIRLE ASÍ A USTED MI CORAZÓN
PERO SI NO LO SACO DE MI PECHO
MUY PRONTO PERDERÉ YO LA RAZÓN

CREO QUE LA AMARÉ MI VIDA ENTERA
AUNQUE ESTE AMOR ME CAUSE GRAN DOLOR
CON PENA LE PIDO QUE SEA SINCERA
AL DECIRME QUE PIENSA DE MI AMOR

NO QUIERO QUE SU AMOR LE CAUSE PENA-
ME DIJO CUANDO YO LE PREGUNTÉ
-HACE MUCHOS AÑOS QUE SOY AJENA
PUES YO TAMBIÉN DE USTED ME ENAMORÉ-

FELIZ YO ME SENTÍ AL ESCUCHARLA
NO PUDE CONTENER MI EMOCIÓN
ME PUSE A ABRAZARLA Y A BESARLA
CUMPLIENDO ASÍ PARTE DE MI ILUSIÓN

AHORA CON MI AMORCITO A MI LADO
DESPUÉS DE QUE ANTE DIOS NOS UNIMOS
RECUERDO CUANTO NOS HEMOS AMADO
DESDE EL PRIMER DÍA QUE NOS CONOCIMOS

BENDITO MI DIOS POR HABERME DADO
AQUEL VALOR QUE ME ARRIMÓ A MI AMADA
PUES SÉ QUE SI NO LE HUBIERA HABLADO
HOY NO ESTUVIERA CONMIGO CASADA

ME SIENTO POR MI DIOS FAVORECIDO
PORQUE AL UNIR NUESTROS CORAZONES
ME REGALÓ A QUIEN MÁS HE QUERIDO
CUMPLIENDO ASÍ TODAS MIS ILUSIONES

TERESITA

TERESITA SE LLAMA MI AMADA
TERESITA SE LLAMA MI AMOR
ES MI ESPOSA, MI AMANTE ADORADA
A MI VIDA LE HA DADO SABOR

JUNTITOS YA CINCUENTA Y CINCO AÑOS
ME HA DADO HIJOS, ME HA DADO CALOR
A MI LADO HA HABIDO DESENGAÑOS
PERO TAMBIÉN MUCHÍSIMO AMOR

TERESITA, ERES MI GRAN TESORO
YO SIN TI YA NO PUEDO VIVIR
ERES BUENA Y POR ESO TE ADORO
GRAN PASIÓN POR TI ME HACES SENTIR

TE DOY GRACIAS PORQUE TÚ ME HAS DADO
UN CARIÑO Y AMOR DE VERDAD
TANTOS AÑOS EN QUE ME HAS BRINDADO
GRAN AMOR Y GRAN FELICIDAD

TERESITA, QUIERO QUE DIOSITO
NO NOS DEJE VIVIR MUCHO MÁS
QUE NOS LLEVE CON EL MUY PRONTITO
QUE MUY PRONTO NOS DIGA —NO MÁS-

SI PRONTO A SU LADO NOS LLAMA
Y UN RINCÓN EN SU TRONO NOS DA
NI LA MUERTE APAGARÁ LA LLAMA
MÁS AMOR HABRÁ EN EL MÁS ALLÁ

AY, DIOSITO, QUÉ LINDA ES LA VIDA
CUANDO TIENE UNO UN CARIÑO ASÍ
NO HE SENTIDO JAMÁS UNA HERIDA
DE LAS QUE ME HAS MANDADO TÚ A MÍ

QUE ESTA DICHA QUE EN EL ALMA SIENTO
NUNCA, NUNCA SE VAYA A ACABAR
QUE DE SU AMOR SIGA YO SEDIENTO
Y QUE NUNCA ME DEJE DE AMAR

SOY UN FRACASADO

QUÉ BUENO PA' NADA HE SIDO YO SIEMPRE
LLEGAR A MI META SE ME HA ESCAPADO
EMPIEZO LAS COSAS CON UN GRAN EMPEÑO
PERO HAY UN TROPIEZO Y LLEGA LA DERROTA

MÚSICA EN LAS VENAS SIEMPRE ME HA CORRIDO
AUNQUE LO HAGO BIEN, VERGÜENZA ME SOBRA
PERO EN ESTE RAMO VERGÜENZA NO AYUDA
EL SUEÑO HA ESCAPADO, PUES YA ESTOY ANCIANO

QUE ALGUIEN INTERPRETE LO QUE YO PRODUZCO
ES AHORA EL GRAN SUEÑO EN MI DECADENCIA
MAS CREO COMO ANTES, QUE SOY UN MEDIOCRE
QUE FALTA EL TALENTO, LA CHISPA QUE CUENTA

SER SEÑOR DE LETRAS FUE OTRO GRAN SUEÑO
ME PUSE EN CAMINO ESTUDIANDO UN TIEMPO
ENVIÉ ALGUNOS CUENTOS ESPERANDO GRAN COSA
FUERON RECHASADOS, PERDÍ LA ESPERANZA

LA ÚNICA META QUE UN DÍA ME FORGÉ
ENSEÑAR AL NIÑO LO POCO QUE SÉ
CON MUCHOS GANÉ, CON OTROS PERDÍ
PERO SATISFECHO QUEDÉ EN ESE FIN

ESPERO MI OTOÑO SE HAGA PRIMAVERA
QUE UNO DE MIS SUEÑOS SE HAGA REALIDAD
CONTENTO ME IRÍA SI ESTO SUCEDIERA
NO QUIERO QUE DIGAN QUE FUI UN FRACASADO

EL SUEÑO REALIZADO

SU LUGAR DE NACIMIENTO, LA HACIENDA DE SAN ANTONIO
A LA EDAD DE SIETE AÑOS DE PADRE YA HUERFANITO
YO CREO QUE LA MALA SUERTE SE LA TRAJO EL DEMONIO
LE HIZO FRENTE A LA VIDA SIENDO AÚN MUY JOVENCITO

A TRABAJAR EN LOS CAMPOS, LO MANDARON MUY DE PRISA
TUVO QUE DEJAR LA ESCUELA, AUNQUE MUCHO LE GUSTABA
SI NO ENCONTRABA TRABAJO, LE DABAN BUENA CUARTIZA
SÓLO ESTANDO TRABAJANDO CONTENTA SU MADRE ESTABA

PASARON SOLO DOS AÑOS Y A SU SUEÑO SE AFERRABA
EL REGRESAR A LA ESCUELA MUY A MENUDO SOÑABA
PUES LA VIDA QUE LLEVABA A NADA LO CONDUCÍA
SABÍA QUE MUY JOVENCITO LA CHAMBA LO MATARÍA

REGRESARON DESDE EL NORTE ALGUNOS DE SUS PAISANOS
CONTANDO DE SUS HAZAÑAS PARA TODOS LOS OÍDOS
OYERON Y DECIDIERON SU MADRE Y SUS HERMANOS
PROBAR SU SUERTE EN EL NORTE, EN LOS ESTADOS UNIDOS

CRUZARON BIEN LA FRONTERA, ENTRE LOS POCHOS VIVIERON
ENTRE LOS CUATRO PENSARON GANAR MUCHOS DOLARITOS
—NO HAY TRABAJO PARA NIÑOS— A SU MADRE LE DIJERON
MANDA A TODOS A LA ESCUELA PA' QUE NO QUEDEN TONTITOS

ESOS TRABAJOS DEL CAMPO AL JOVEN SE LE OLVIDARON
AQUEL SUEÑO QUE TENÍA SE LE IBA A REALIZAR
A LA VIDA DE LOS POCHOS PRONTO SE ACOSTUMBRARON
HASTA EL ESPAÑOL QUE HABLABAN SE LES LLEGÓ A OLVIDAR

AL CURSAR LA SECUNDARIA, SU ESPAÑOL LO AVERGONZABA
FUE MEJORANDO SU IDIOMA EN LA UNIVERSIDAD
NO HABLAR BIEN EL ESPAÑOL EN EL ALMA LE PESABA
PUES QUERÍA HABLARLO BIEN, HABLARLO BIEN DE VERDAD

YA ES MAESTRO JUBILADO, CONSIGUIÓ LO QUE QUERÍA
EN HABLAR EL ESPAÑOL UN POQUITO HA MEJORADO
AUNQUE ALLÁ EN MEXICALI POCA ES SU MEJORÍA
HABLANDO CON LOS LOCALES QUEDA POCO AVERGONZADO

AHORA ÉL ESCRIBE CANCIONES QUE LO HACEN RECORDAR
AQUELLA NIÑEZ MUY TRISTE QUE QUISIERA YA OLVIDAR
CON TODITAS SUS CANCIONES ÉL SE PONE A PENSAR
QUE DE QUEHACERES DEL CAMPO, SÓLO LE GUSTA CANTAR

SÉ HUMANO Y DE BUEN CORAZÓN

CUANDO TÚ A TU HERMANO HAS MIRADO
A LA GENTE UNA AYUDA PIDIENDO
EN SEGUIDA MUY MAL LO HAS JUSGADO
—SINVERGÜENZA- TE AGARRAS DICIENDO
—PEREZOSO QUE VIVE DE GORRA
ÉL SE IRÁ SIN QUE YO LO SOCORRA-

SE REPITE ESTA ESCENA SEGUIDO
EL EXTIENDE SU MANO AL MIRARTE
TU REACCIÓN LA MISMA SIEMPRE HA SIDO
—YO NINGÚN CENTAVO VOY A DARTE
VE Y TRABAJA, NO SEAS MANTENIDO
NADA DOY, YA TE LO HE REPETIDO-

SI ALGUNA GRACIA DIOS TE HA MANDADO
ES PARA QUE ASÍ ENSALCES SU NOMBRE
RECUERDA QUE AL SER ASÍ DOTADO
TÚ TAMBIÉN GANARÁS GRAN RENOMBRE
PERO SI CON ÉLLA ERES TACAÑO
ANTE DIOS BAJARÁS DE TAMAÑO

NO HAY NADA PEOR QUE UN AGARRADO
CON COSAS QUE PUEDE COMPARTIR
PUES DIOSITO ESAS COSAS LE HA DADO
PARA VER SI SABE BIEN VIVIR
SI SE LAS NIEGA AL QUE VA A PEDIR
DE SEGURO SU ALMA VA A MORIR

MUCHA GENTE HAY DESAFORTUNADA
QUE EN LA CALLE SE PASA LA VIDA
CON GRAN FE EN SU DIOS, SIN TENER NADA
HAMBRIENTOS, QUE TIENEN POR COMIDA
BANQUETES O MIGAJAS EN MANO
SEGÚN EL GRAN AMOR DE SU HERMANO

CUANDO VEAS A UN HAMBRIENTO O SEDIENTO
SÉ HUMANO Y DE BUEN CORAZÓN
QUIZÁS DIOS SE DISFRAZA DE HAMBRIENTO
PARA VER SI TIENES COMPASIÓN
RECUERDA QUE EL QUE DA LO QUE TIENE
RECOMPENSA DEL CIELO LE VIENE

AL MIRAR A UN MENDIGO, HAS PENSADO
QUIÉN LE DIO ESA VIDA DE MENDIGO
MIENTRAS A TI TODITO TE HA DADO
NUESTRO DIOS FUE EL QUE SE LA HA ESCOGIDO
CON EL FIN DE LLEVÁRSELO AL CIELO
CUANDO SU CUERPO ESTE BAJO SUELO

AMOR Y MÁS AMOR

ENAMORADO CUATRO VECES HE ESTADO
NO POR TODAS FUI QUERIDO
POR DOS SÍ ME SENTÍ MUY AMADO
POR LAS OTRAS QUEDÉ HERIDO

DE LAS DOS QUE ME CORRESPONDIERON
UNA FUE CUANDO PEQUEÑO
AUNQUE LAS DOS GRAN AMOR ME DIERON
DE UNA AL FIN FUI SU DUEÑO

A LOS DOCE AÑOS ES INFATUACIÓN
PORQUE ES UNO INOCENTE
YA MADURO SE ENTREGA EL CORAZÓN
Y EL AMOR NO ES TAN DECENTE

NO SÓLO SE ENTREGA EL CORAZÓN
Y TODAS LAS EMOCIONES
SE ENTREGA UNO DEL TODO A UN MONTÓN
Y PIERDE HASTA LOS CALZONES

CUANDO DE VERDAD ME ENAMORÉ
VEINTISIETE AÑOS TENÍA
A ÉSTA DE CORAZÓN LA ADORÉ
Y LA ADORO TODAVÍA

ÉSTA ÚLTIMA SÍ ES MUY BELLA
Y ES MUJER MUY ADMIRABLE
ES MÁS LINDA QUE CUALQUIER ESTRELLA
Y ES COMPLETAMENTE ADORABLE

PORQUE ESTABAMOS ENAMORADOS
PRONTO FUIMOS A CASARNOS
CINCUENTA Y CINCO AÑOS DE CASADOS
Y NO DEJAMOS DE AMARNOS

A UN PRINCIPIO EN MIS AMORES
NO CUMPLÍ CON MIS DEBERES
MAS CUANDO CORREGÍ MIS ERRORES
TUVE ÉXITO EN MIS QUERERES

AMORÍOS TUVIMOS CON CLAMOR
CON MUCHÍSIMA FRECUENCIA
COMPATIBILIDAD EN EL AMOR
TUVO EN ESO MUCHA INFLUENCIA

ESOS AMORÍOS SE ESFUMARON
POR UN MAL MUY CANCEROSO
POR EL MAL DE CANCER ME QUITARON
EN AMORÍOS LO VIRTUOSO

PERO NUESTRO AMOR SIGUE FUERTE
MAS YA NO ES TEMPESTUOSO
AUNQUE EL FUEGO YA ES INERTE
NUESTRO AMOR AÚN ES HERMOSO

A PESAR DE SER POCO PACIENTE
DE CARICIAS ES DOTADO
AUNQUE NO TENGA NADA DE ARDIENTE
ES AÚN FUERTE Y CALMADO

PROBLEMAS DE SALUD NOS ABRUMAN
QUE OPACAN NUESTRA ALEGRÍA
POR NUESTRA EDAD YA NO SE ESFUMAN
Y NOS DURA TODO EL DÍA

VIVIREMOS ASÍ CON ESE MAL
HASTA QUE EL SEÑOR NOS LLAME
CON ESOS DOLORES HASTA EL FINAL
SERÁ UNA VIDA INFAME

POR NUESTRO AMOR AGUANTAREMOS
ESTA VIDA TAN INFAME
PERO MUY PRONTO DESCANSAREMOS
CUANDO EL SEÑOR NOS LLAME

¿HE LOGRADO MIS METAS?

¿QUÉ ES LO QUE QUISE HACER?
O MÁS BIEN ME DEBO PREGUNTAR,
¿QUÉ ES LO QUE DEBERÍA HABER HECHO?
NO SÉ SI FUE UNA OPCIÓN O UN DEBER
QUE DIOSITO QUISO DARME,
O SI LO LLEGUÉ UN DÍA A LOGRAR,
O TERMINÓ EN GRAN DESPECHO.
NUNCA EN MI LARGA VIDA VOY
EN REALIDAD A LLEGARLO A SABER,
PUES CON MUCHAS DUDAS ESTOY.

EN TODO LO QUE HICE GANAS LE PUSE.
CON MUCHAS GANAS DE TRIUNFAR,
HACER MUCHAS COSAS LO INTENTÉ.
MAS NO SÉ SI LO LOGRÉ.
MI META FUE DURO TRABAJAR
Y ESE TRABAJO ME IMPUSE.
DESDE MUY NIÑO PENSÉ,
Y CON MUCHAS GANAS DESEÉ,
LLEGAR A SER PROFESIONAL CANTANTE.
PERO EL TIEMPO RÁPIDO SE FUE
Y EL TRIUNFO QUEDÓ DISTANTE.

LUEGO INTENTÉ ESCRIBIR
CUENTOS PARA A NIÑOS DIVERTIR.
MAS ESE INTENTO TAMBIÉN FRACASÓ,
PUES MI TRABAJO NO MUCHO SE VENDIÓ.
EL TRIUNFO SE ESCAPÓ Y DESILUSIONADO QUEDE
QUIZÁS MI TALENTO NO FUE BASTANTE
O MI ALIENTO ME FALTÓ.
SEA LO QUE HAYA SIDO, ESE INTENTO ME FALLÓ

ENTONCES ME VINO A LA MENTE
ESCRIBIR ALGUNAS CANCIONES.
Y PUEDO DECIR QUE DE REPENTE
QUISE CUMPLIR MIS INTENCIONES.
MÁS DE SETECIENTAS HE ESCRITO,
MAS AHÍ QUEDARON MIS ILUSIONES.
PERO SIEMPRE HE PENSADO Y DICHO
QUE, SIN APOYO NI CONECCIONES,
NO SE CUMPLE SINGÚN CAPRICHO,
Y SE VAN ABAJO LAS BUENAS INTENCIONES.

YO LE LLAMO FRACASO ROTUNDO
A TODITOS MIS PASADOS INTENTOS.
AUNQUE ALGUNOS EN EL MUNDO,
CON MIS TALENTOS ESTÁN CONTENTOS.
A MI MENTE LUEGO ME VINO
A ESCRIBIR POEMAS ENTRARLE.
YA HE ESCRITO UN MONTÓN,
UNOS LARGOS Y OTROS MÁS CORTITOS.
A TODOS CALIDAD DE POEMAS QUISE DARLES
PERO UNO U OTRO SE CONVIRTIÓ EN CANCIÓN

DURANTE TODOS ESTOS INTENTOS,
A UNA COSA LE PUSE MÁS FERVOR.
A HACERME MAESTRO DE NIÑOS ME ENFOQUÉ.
A ESO EN TODOS MOMENTOS LE PUSE TODO MI AMOR
DESPUÉS DE CUARENTA AÑOS,
LA VIDA DE MUCHOS NIÑOS TOQUÉ.
CON ALUMNOS DE MUCHOS TAMAÑOS,
DE TRABAJAR TUVE EL PLACER.
CON MUCHO PLACER Y CARIÑO,
A ESTUDIAR LOS PUDE ALENTAR

A ESTUDIAR LOS PUDE ALENTAR.
Y AUNQUE SEA CON UN GRANITO DE ARENA,
ESPERO QUE A MÁS QUE A UN NIÑO,
O QUIZÁS A MÁS DE UNA DOCENA,
LES HAYA AYUDADO A TRIUNFAR.
CREO QUE DE ESO SÍ ORGULLOSO PUEDO ESTAR.
VARIOS TRIUNFADORES LAS GRACIAS ME HAN DADO
POR EL SAFISFACTORIO BIENESTAR
QUE CON MI AYUDA HAN LOGRADO.

PARA TERMINAR, QUIERO ENTREGAR
LAS GRACIAS A MI DIOSITO
PORQUE HE LLEGADO A LOGRAR
UN ÉXITO, AUNQUE SEA CHIQUITO.
NO SÓLO EN EL CANTO FRACASÉ
SINO EN LOS CUENTOS Y POEMAS TAMBIÉN.
PERO ESTOY SEGURO, Y LO SÉ,
QUE EN LA EDUCACIÓN SÍ LOGRÉ
HACERLE A MUCHOS EL BIEN.

MIL GRACIAS POR SU VIDA

SE FUE ÉLLA CAMINANDO
PENSANDO REGRESAR
YO ME QUEDÉ ESPERANDO
CON PIENSOS DE GOZAR
SU GRATA COMPAÑÍA
A ÉLLA ACOSTMBRADO
PERO YA PRESENTÍA
QUE ALGO LE HABÍA PASADO

PASÉ HORAS ESPANTOSAS
TRISTE Y DESESPERADO
PENSANDO HORRIBLES COSAS
QUE LE HABRÍAN SUCEDIDO
MI MENTE ME DECÍA
QUE DIOS LA HABÍA LLAMADO
TRISTEMENTE CREÍA
QUE LA HABÍA YA PERDIDO

LE DIJE A DIOS BENDITO
--AYÚDAME UN POQUITO
TE PIDO UN MILAGRITO
REGRESA A MI AMORCITO
NO LA DEJES SOLITA
EN SU TERRIBLE TRANCE
HAZ QUE LA VIRGENCITA
CON PROTECCIÓN LA ALCANCE--

PASÓ YA EL SUFRIMIENTO
YA REGRESÓ A MIS BRAZOS
¡CUÁN GRANDE EL SENTIMIENTO
QUE AL VERLA YO SENTÍA!
ANSIABA PROTEGERLA
CUBRIRLA CON ABRAZOS
DESPUÉS DE HORAS SIN VERLA
CONMIGO LA TENÍA

MI DIOS HIZO POSIBLE
EL HABER TRANSFORMADO
UNA ANGUSTIA TERRIBLE
EN DICHA Y ALEGRÍA
¡QUÉ ALIVIO HABÍA SENTIDO
AL VERLA AQUÍ A MI LADO!
PUES ÉL HA PERMITIDO
QUE SIGA SIENDO MÍA

DIOS TODOPODEROSO
TE ESTOY AGRADECIDO
HAS SIDO MUY PIADOSO
CON MI MUJER QUERIDA
UN MILAGRO ME HICISTE
AUNQUE NO MERECIDO
A MI AMADA TRAJISTE
MIL GRACIAS POR SU VIDA

ABOUT THE AUTHOR

He was born in Mexico, came to the U. S. in 1945 illegally, became legal in 1955, was drafted after one year of college, served almost two years with the Army's Special Troops in Germany, was released from the army and rerturned to Imperial Valley College, went on to San Diego State University, graduating with a Bachelor's Degree in Liberal Studies and a Master's Degree in Bilingual Education, taught elementary school grades 5th through 8th for 34 years and subbed in Kinder through 4th grades for six years. He also took a course in Children's Literature and, after writing three short stories, quit when assigned a regular, full-length novel that required research, which he felt he did not have time to do because of my full-time teaching duties plus my night-time teaching of English to adults.

Printed in the United States
By Bookmasters